IBM WEBSPHERE

Frequently Asked Questions

[Compiled and Edited by Terry Sanchez-Clark]

IBM WEBSPHERE Frequently Asked Questions

ISBN: 978-1-60332-008-5

Edited By: Jamie Fisher

Printed in the United States of America

Please visit our website at www.ibmcookbook.com

Table of Contents

Introduction

WebSphere refers to a brand of IBM software products, although the term also popularly refers to one specific product: WebSphere Application Server (WAS). WebSphere helped define the middleware software category and is designed to set up, operate and integrate e-business applications across multiple computing platforms using Web technologies. It includes both the run-time components (like WAS) and the tools to develop applications that will run on WAS.

The WebSphere Business Integration Server offers to facilitate the following business needs:

1. Process Automation - Coordinates business process activities that span multiple applications, which may be geographically local or remote, internal or external to an organization.
2. Process and Workforce Management - Coordinates long-lived activities that span multiple systems and workforce groups. Avoid bottlenecks by automating and managing task list assignment, rather than specific emails to individuals.
3. Application Integration - Coordinates information flows by transformation, distribution and enrichment of in-flight messages across the enterprise.
4. Application Connectivity - Connect applications, technologies, industry standards, data sources, and mainframes within and outside the enterprise.
5. Integrated Visual Tooling - Manage, design, test, and deploy business process solutions in a team development environment.

With WebSphere Business Integration Modeler V5.1, you can complete the following key modeling activities:

1. Graphically model your current and potential business processes
2. View your models as 'swimlanes' to see how each resource you use relates to the activities in your model
3. Perform simulations to see how your processes will perform under different "what if" scenarios and environmental conditions

4. Analyze the simulation results to determine how to correct problem areas in your models, such as bottlenecks and workload imbalances
5. Generate reports from your models or simulation results using a wide variety of predefined report templates, or create your own custom reports
6. Create and update models with other team members using the team support and versioning capabilities of Business Integration Modeler
7. Print your models or reports to communicate and share the information within your organization
8. Publish models to the Web for information sharing purposes
9. Import Microsoft® Visio data as the basis or starting point for your model development
10. Jump-start your application development process by exporting your completed models to BPEL, WSDL, and XSD format, and then importing them into IBM WebSphere Studio Application Developer, Integration Edition for Linux and Windows® V5.1
11. Create workflow automation solutions from your models by exporting your completed models to FDL format, and then importing them into IBM WebSphere MQ Workflow Buildtime V3.5
12. Export your models to IBM Rational XDE for further refinement

But WebSphere Business Integration Modeler V5.1 is more than just a graphical modeling tool. It provides powerful simulation and analysis capabilities, which enable businesses to observe how their current processes perform and how they will respond to a variety of "what if" conditions, and then analyze the results to pinpoint weaknesses, such as bottlenecks to help reduce costs and generate more profit.

For businesses that are looking to move their models into the implementation phase, WebSphere Business Integration Modeler provides the exporting capabilities to transform finished models into the technology required for their business solutions, including BPEL, WSDL, and XSD for developing WebSphere Business Integration Server Foundation applications from the models, FDL for developing workflow automation solutions, or UML for further refining the models in IBM Rational XDE.

Business Integration Modeler provides three different user profiles to meet the modeling needs of a wide variety of users.

Each profile exposes a different level of modeling detail to suit different modeling needs.

1. The Basic Business Modeling profile is intended for the business analyst or other user who wants to work at the high-level view of a business process model. This profile focuses on creating and displaying sequence flows and does not expose low-level technical details of process and data modeling.

2. The Intermediate Business Modeling profile gives the more technically focused user the opportunity to specify and view additional details of process and data models. For example, with this profile you can specify business rules and logic that apply to model elements and a broader set of specifications for data attributes.

3. The Advanced Business Modeling profile provides the most comprehensive level of detail for process models and data models. This profile facilitates the work of technically experienced personnel who prepare models that will be used as the basis for software applications. For example, you can use this profile to specify invocation characteristics, static fields, instance correlations, and a larger set of simulation parameters.

WebSphere Business Integration Modeler Advanced Edition V5.1 likewise offers three different technology modes so that you can develop the models in the run-time environment in which you will later deploy them. Each technology mode exposes only the functionality permitted in that run-time environment.

1. The **BPEL technology mode** is optimized for exporting models to Business Process Execution Language (BPEL) format, which you can then import into WebSphere Studio Application Developer Integration Edition, where you can further define the process for deploying to IBM WebSphere Business Integration Server Foundation V5.1.

2. The **MQ Workflow FDL technology mode** is optimized for exporting models to Flow Definition Language (FDL) format, which you can then use in WebSphere MQ Workflow V3.5 as the basis of an automated workflow solution.

3. The **Operational technology mode** provides the most comprehensive detail of the three technology modes. This technology mode is ideal for developing

business models that are not targeted for deployment to the above runtime environments.

WebSphere Business Integration Modeler V5.1 is built using the Eclipse open source technology, allowing it to integrate and inter-operate with other Eclipse-based IBM tools, such as IBM WebSphere Studio Application Developer, Integration Edition for Linux and Windows, Version 5.1 on Windows.

With what types of files can you import into WebSphere Business Integration Modeler 5.1?

You can successfully import the following types of files:

1. FDL files (files developed in WebSphere MQ Workflow Buildtime 3.5)
2. ADF files (WebSphere Business Integration Workbench 4.2.4 models)
3. Delimited text files (to import data from other programs, such as spreadsheets or databases)
4. XSD files (XML Schema Definition)
5. VDX files (Visio files created in Microsoft Visio 2002 or 2003)
6. Business Integration Modeler V5 Projects (files created in Business Integration Modeler V5.1)

Question 1: WebSphere Business Integration Modeler Entry Edition v5.1 and WebSphere Business Integration Modeler Advanced Edition V5.1

What is the difference between WebSphere Business Integration Modeler Entry Edition V5.1 and WebSphere Business Integration Modeler Advanced Edition V5.1?

A: WebSphere Business Integration Entry Edition Version 5.1 is a low cost option for business users who are looking for a simple and easy-to-use tool to model, document, and print their business processes.

WebSphere Business Integration Advanced Edition Version 5.1 provides all the capabilities of the Entry Edition. In addition, it enables business users to perform complex simulations on their process models based on "what if" scenarios and then analyze and generate reports from the simulation results to identify problem areas in the processes, such as bottlenecks. The Advanced Edition also provides a "jump-start" to application development by enabling more technically focused users, such as IT architects, to export the models to BPEL, UML, or FDL models, for further refinement.

The following table summarizes the key functional differences between the Entry and Advanced Editions:

Feature	Modeler Entry Edition	Modeler Advanced Edition
Modeling Profiles	Basic, Intermediate, Advanced	Basic, Intermediate, Advanced
Editing modes	Operational	Operational, BPEL, FDL
Teaming (check-in/check-out)	Yes	Yes
Simulation	No	Yes
Static and Dynamic Analysis	No	Yes
Reporting (create	Yes	Yes

reports)

- Query	Yes	Yes
- Basis Report Templates (available)	Yes	Yes
Printing	Yes	Yes
Modeler Project Import/Export	Yes	Yes
Delimited file Import/Export	Yes	Yes
ADF Import	Yes	Yes
XSD Import/Export	No	Yes
UML Export	No	Yes
FDL and BPEL Export	No	Yes
FDL Import	No	Yes

Question 2: Importing Microsoft Visio files into WebSphere

Can one import Microsoft Visio files into WebSphere Business Integration Modeler 5.1?

A: Yes, you can import shapes from Microsoft Visio 2002 or 2003 files into WebSphere Business Integration Modeler V5.1. These shapes can be used to create elements such as tasks and business items in WebSphere Business Integration Modeler.

Question 3: Export formats

When I have completed my models, what formats or applications can I export them to?

A: You can export models created in WebSphere Business Integration Modeler Advanced Edition V5.1 to the following file formats:

1. BPEL, WSDL, and XSD, to import into IBM WebSphere Studio Application Developer, Integration Edition for Linux and Windows V5.1; and later deploy to WebSphere Business Integration Server Foundation V5.1
2. UML, to import into Rational® XDE™
3. FDL Business Modeling Profile, to import into IBM WebSphere MQ Workflow Buildtime V3.5
4. Delimited text format (business items only)
5. Business Integration Modeler V5 Project format, to back up or share Modeler V5 projects

Question 4: Admin Console Access

After federating a node with an application server into the Deployment manager, I am unable to access the admin console of the application server but I can access the admin console of the Deployment Manager. Is this how it is supposed to be? Does access to the admin console of the application server get blocked when you federate it with a NDM?

What is the explanation for this?

A: Yes, it does get blocked. Once you federate the base to the network deployment, the control will then be from the Network deployment. There will be a node agent installed on the Base that the DMGR in the network deployment communicate to.

Question 5: Websphere V5.0 Security Issue

I am running a WAS 5.0 base deployment on Solaris with a single application server. When I turn the Global security on, I had the problem of stopping the server. Could anyone help me how to stop the server?

A: You have to stop the server using the user and password, which you use when you enabled the global security.

Go to install_root/bin directory of the WebSphere Application Server installation or a Network Deployment installation. Generally on uix
/opt/WebSphere/AppServer/bin /stopServer.sh server1
windows:
C:\program files\IBM\WebSphere\AppServer\bin \stopServer.bat server1

Syntax:
```
stopServer <server> [options]
```

UNIX:
```
stopServer.sh <server_name> -user <name_of_the_user>
-password <given_password>

stopServer.sh server1 -user jones -password jones123
```

Windows:
```
stopServer.bat <server_name> -user <name_of_the_user>
-password <given_password>

stopServer.bat server1 -user jones -password jones123
```

Question 6: WebSphere + Tivoli Directory Server: Web Admin Tool problems

I use WebSphere 6.0 and am trying to use Tivoli Directory Server 6.0 with it. Installation as well as the creation of server and database went okay. In the WebSphere's Admin Console, I added IDSWebApp to the list of applications and it starts normally. But when I try logging in to Tivoli's Web Administration Tool, in the list of available hostnames, I get only "Console Admin"; logging in with superadmin+secret works.

The problem is that the two page "change admin login" and "change admin pwd" are blank and on the "manage console servers" and "manage console properties", I get nothing but two NoSuchMethodError-Exceptions that are listed below. I tried re-installing Tivoli, deactivating WebSphere's Global Security, and installing Tivoli's Fixpack (6.0.0.9), but nothing changed.

The content of the page "Manage console servers" are as follows:

```
Exception #0
java.lang.NoSuchMethodError:
com.ibm.psw.wcl.components.table.WTable: method

getResourceBundle(Ljava/util/Locale;)Ljava/util/Resou
rceBundle; not found
at
com.ibm.mdr.wcl.DrTableCreator.create(DrTableCreator.
java:483)
at
com.ibm.mdr.DrCreatorFactory.recurseData(DrCreatorFac
tory.java:112)
at
com.ibm.mdr.DrContainerCreator.recurseChildren(DrCont
ainerCreator.java:97)
at
com.ibm.mdr.wcl.DrDatagroupCreator.create(DrDatagroup
Creator.java:362)
at
com.ibm.mdr.DrCreatorFactory.recurseData(DrCreatorFac
tory.java:112)
at
com.ibm.mdr.DrCreatorFactory.createStateTree(DrCreato
rFactory.java:77)
at
com.ibm.mdr.DrStateMgr.createStateTree(DrStateMgr.jav
```

```
a:1003)
at
com.ibm.mdr.DrStateMgr.invoke(DrStateMgr.java:2539)
at
com.ibm.mdr.DrRendererManager.invoke(DrRendererManage
r.java:377)
at
com.ibm.mdr.DrRenderer.invoke(DrRenderer.java:1240)
at
com.ibm.ui.framework.UserTaskManager.invoke(UserTaskM
anager.java:1361)
at
com.ibm.ui.framework.UserTaskManager.invoke(UserTaskM
anager.java:1322)
at
com.ibm.ldap.IDSAdmin.ConsoleServersPanel.init(Consol
eServersPanel.java:123)
at
com.ibm.webnav.servlet.WnTransactionManager.processTr
ansaction(WnTransactionManager.java:580)
at
com.ibm.webnav.servlet.WnTransactionThread.run(WnTran
sactionThread.java:111)
```

The content of the page "Manage console properties":

```
Exception #0
java.lang.NoSuchMethodError:
com.ibm.psw.wcl.components.table.WTable: method

getResourceBundle(Ljava/util/Locale;)Ljava/util/Resou
rceBundle; not found
at
com.ibm.mdr.wcl.DrTableCreator.create(DrTableCreator.
java:483)
at
com.ibm.mdr.DrCreatorFactory.recurseData(DrCreatorFac
tory.java:112)
at
com.ibm.mdr.DrContainerCreator.recurseChildren(DrCont
ainerCreator.java:97)
at
com.ibm.mdr.wcl.DrGroupCreator.create(DrGroupCreator.
java:224)
at
com.ibm.mdr.DrCreatorFactory.recurseData(DrCreatorFac
tory.java:112)
at
com.ibm.mdr.DrContainerCreator.recurseChildren(DrCont
ainerCreator.java:97)
```

```
at
com.ibm.mdr.wcl.DrGroupCreator.create(DrGroupCreator.
java:224)
at
com.ibm.mdr.DrCreatorFactory.recurseData(DrCreatorFac
tory.java:112)
at
com.ibm.mdr.wcl.DrGroupCreator.recurseSelectableChild
ren(DrGroupCreator.java:709)
at
com.ibm.mdr.wcl.DrDatagroupCreator.create(DrDatagroup
Creator.java:353)
at
com.ibm.mdr.DrCreatorFactory.recurseData(DrCreatorFac
tory.java:112)
at
com.ibm.mdr.DrCreatorFactory.createStateTree(DrCreato
rFactory.java:77)
at
com.ibm.mdr.DrStateMgr.createStateTree(DrStateMgr.jav
a:1003)
at
com.ibm.mdr.DrStateMgr.invoke(DrStateMgr.java:2539)
at
com.ibm.mdr.DrRendererManager.invoke(DrRendererManage
r.java:377)
at
com.ibm.mdr.DrRenderer.invoke(DrRenderer.java:1240)
at
com.ibm.ui.framework.UserTaskManager.invoke(UserTaskM
anager.java:1361)
at
com.ibm.ui.framework.UserTaskManager.invoke(UserTaskM
anager.java:1322)
at
com.ibm.ldap.IDSAdmin.ConsolePropertiesPanel.init(Con
solePropertiesPanel.java:123)
at
com.ibm.webnav.servlet.WnTransactionManager.processTr
ansaction(WnTransactionManager.java:580)
at
com.ibm.webnav.servlet.WnTransactionThread.run(WnTran
sactionThread.java:111)
```

How can I resolve this problem?

A: A good workaround for your problem is that instead of forcing an installation of Tivoli Directory Server in the already installed WebSphere Application Server, use the embedded version of WAS that comes along with the TDS. It is already configured for TDS. This means that you will have your WebSphere Portal Server running using the original WAS, and on the other hand, TDS runs on top of its embedded version of WAS.

Apparently, this is a waste of system resources and a possible cause for compatibility problems (2 WAS running), but it seems the best solution because the embedded WAS does not slow down the system, loads rapidly, does not get in conflict with the other WAS and you have the possibility to administer TDS independently from WebSphere.

Furthermore, if you plan your system wisely, you should use a dedicated server machine for WebSphere and another one for TDS, and in this case you are forced to use an Application Server on every machine.

Question 7: Out of memory problem

I would like to know the steps to follow to resolve an out of memory problem on a system with Websphere running on it.

Is there some advice or suggestion I can work on?

A: For your specific problem, go and visit the following site for explanations:
http://www.bmc.com/products/documents/70/31/57031/57031
.pdf#search=%22out%20of%20memory%20websphere%22

Quote from the website cited:

"Garbage Collection Duration Parameter

It displays the average amount of time (over the given discovery cycle) JVM spent cleaning up unused portions of memory. This parameter:

> Is updated every five minutes.
> Is accessed by selecting WebSphere icon -> JVM server icon -> Server Resources -> Garbage
Collection Duration.

JVM is in charge of gathering and reusing free memory because the J2EE specification frees the
JAVA programmer from that task. Garbage collection is the process of JVM that frees unused
portions of memory and returns the portions to the heap size.

Garbage collection is good and bad:

> Good, because it gives JVM more memory for JVM heap
> Bad, because JVM tends to slow down J2EE transactions during Garbage Collection

Thus, Garbage Collection is a "balancing act." If Garbage Collection does not happen, then JVM runs out of memory. If Garbage Collection happens too often, or takes too long, your JAVA programs slow down. The Garbage Collection Duration should start small and grow over time (since initially JVM does not have a lot of memory to free up).

If your JVM is spending more than 5% of the time in Garbage Collection, you may have a problem. In Figure 4, assuming the Garbage Collection Duration is collected every 5 minutes (300 seconds), a good warning level for this parameter would be 15 seconds."

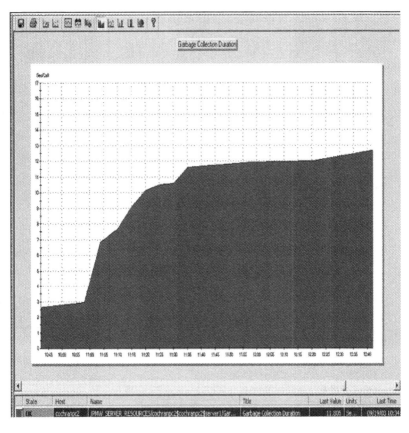

Figure 4: Garbage Collection Duration Parameter

Question 8: Cloning Websphere configuration

We have an environment with one ND machine and two machines running each two Application Servers (vertical and horizontal cluster). There are lots of configuration options set on either the whole cell or single Application servers.

I want to set up one machine containing the ND and two Application servers with cells that have the same configuration as the other cell but different hostname and IP. Backup and restore with backupConfig.sh will not work as far as the documentation says, since it needs to have the same IP/name on restore. I could copy the whole /opt/IBM/ directory structure to the new machine and grep/sed the name/IP to the new one, but I guess that won't work.

What would be the best way to clone the configuration of a Websphere 6 with ND? Could anyone suggest some other ideas on how to do it?

A: WAS 6 supports cloning of configuration from one server to other.

<u>Exporting and importing profiles</u>

WebSphere Application Server V6 provides a mechanism that allows you to export certain profiles, or server objects from a profile, to an archive. The archive can be distributed and imported to other installations. An exported archive is a zip file of the configuration directory with host-specific information removed. The recommended extension of the zip file is .car. The exported archive can be the complete configuration or a subset. Importing the archive creates the configurations defined in the archive. The target configuration of an archive export / import can be a specific server or an entire profile.

To use an archive you would:

1. Export a WebSphere configuration. This creates a zip file with the configuration.
2. Unzip the files for browsing or update for use on other systems. For example, you might need to update resource references.

3. Send the configuration to the new system. An import can work with the zip file or with the expanded format.
4. Import the archive. The import process requires that you identify the object in the configuration you want to import and the target object in the existing configuration. The target can be the same object type as the archive or its parent:
   – If you import a server archive to a server configuration the configurations are merged.
   – If you import a server archive to a node, the server is added to the node.

A tutorial on creating and using archives can be found in the Information Center. See ftp://ftp.software.ibm.com/software/eod/WAS_6-0/SystemManagement/Presentations/ WASv6_SM_Configuration_Archives/playershell.swf

Server Archives

The following command can be used to create an archive of a server:

```
$AdminTask exportServer {-archive <archive_location>
-nodeName <node>
-serverName <server>}
```

This process removes applications from the server that you specify, breaks the relationship between the server that you specify and the core group of the server, cluster, or SIBus membership. If you export a single server of a cluster, the relation to the cluster is eliminated.
To import a server archive use the following command:

```
$AdminTask importServer {-archive <archive_location>
[-nodeInArchive <node>]
[-serverInArchive <server>] [-nodeName <node>]
[-serverName <server>]}
```

When you use the importServer command, you select a configuration object in the archive as the source and select a configuration object on the system as the target. The target object can match the source object or be its parent. If the source and target are the same, the configurations are merged.

Profile Archives

The following command can be used to create an archive of a profile:

```
$AdminTask exportWasprofile {-archive
<archive_location>}
```

You can only create an archive of an unfederated profile (standalone application server).

```
$AdminTask importWasprofile {-archive
<archive_location>}
```

Question 9: Configuring plugin-cfg.xml for Load balancing in WAS5.1.1.10

I am trying to do Load Balancing on two Application servers from Apache Webserver. I was partially successful by getting the round robin load balancing. However, the session that I established is not permanent, i.e., for every other click, it points me to the other application server without holding the session.

How do I set up a persistent session with load balancing?

The plugin file I am using is as follows:

```
cat plugin-cfg.xml

<?xml version="1.0" encoding="ISO-8859-1"?>

<Config ASDisableNagle="false"
AcceptAllContent="false"
AppServerPortPreference="HostHeader"
ChunkedResponse="false" FIPSEnable="false"
IISDisableNagle="false" IISPluginPriority="High"
IgnoreDNSFailures="false" RefreshInterval="60"
ResponseChunkSize="64" VHostMatchingCompat="false">
    <Log LogLevel="Trace"
Name="/tmp/http_plugin.log"/>
    <Property Name="ESIEnable" Value="true"/>
    <Property Name="ESIMaxCacheSize" Value="1024"/>
    <Property Name="ESIInvalidationMonitor"
Value="false"/>
    <VirtualHostGroup Name="default_host">
        <VirtualHost Name="*:9080"/>
        <VirtualHost Name="*:80"/>
        <VirtualHost Name="*:9443"/>
        <VirtualHost Name="*:9081"/>
        <VirtualHost Name="*:9444"/>
    </VirtualHostGroup>
    <ServerCluster CloneSeparatorChange="false"
LoadBalance="Round Robin" Name="Testh_Cluster"
PostBufferSize="64" PostSizeLimit="-1"
RemoveSpecialHeaders="true" RetryInterval="60">
        <Server ConnectTimeout="0" CloneID="F1234567"
ExtendedHandshake="false" LoadBalanceWeight="2"
MaxConnections="-1" Name="xxxapp123_server1"
ServerIOTimeout="0" WaitForContinue="false">
            <Transport Hostname="xxxapp123" Port="9080"
Protocol="http"/>
            <Transport Hostname="xxxapp123" Port="9443"
```

```
Protocol="https">
        <Property Name="keyring"
Value="/opt/WebSphere/AppServer/etc/plugin-key.kdb"/>
        <Property Name="stashfile"
Value="/opt/WebSphere/AppServer/etc/plugin-key.sth"/>
      </Transport>
    </Server>
    <Server ConnectTimeout="0" CloneID="F1234568"
ExtendedHandshake="false" LoadBalanceWeight="2"
MaxConnections="-1" Name="xxxapp161_server2"
ServerIOTimeout="0" WaitForContinue="false">
      <Transport Hostname="xxxapp161" Port="9081"
Protocol="http"/>
      <Transport Hostname="xxxapp161" Port="9444"
Protocol="https">
        <Property Name="keyring"
Value="/opt/WebSphere/AppServer/etc/plugin-key.kdb"/>
        <Property Name="stashfile"
Value="/opt/WebSphere/AppServer/etc/plugin-key.sth"/>
      </Transport>
    </Server>
    <PrimaryServers>
      <Server Name="xxxapp161_server2"/>
      <Server Name="xxxapp123_server1"/>
    </PrimaryServers>
  </ServerCluster>
  <UriGroup Name="default_host_Test_Cluster_URIs">
    <Uri AffinityCookie="JSESSIONID"
AffinityURLIdentifier="jsessionid" Name="/pbtwes/*"/>
  </UriGroup>
  <Route ServerCluster="Test_Cluster"
UriGroup="default_host_Test_Cluster_URIs"
VirtualHostGroup="default_host"/>
  <RequestMetrics armEnabled="false"
loggingEnabled="true" rmEnabled="false"
traceLevel="HOPS">
    <filters enable="false" type="URI">
      <filterValues enable="false"
value="/servlet/snoop"/>
      <filterValues enable="false"
value="/webapp/examples/HitCount"/>
    </filters>
    <filters enable="false" type="SOURCE_IP">
      <filterValues enable="false"
value="255.255.255.255"/>
      <filterValues enable="false"
value="254.254.254.254"/>
    </filters>
  </RequestMetrics>
</Config>
```

A: For readings on your problem, see **http://www-128.ibm.com/developerworks/forums/dw_thread.jsp?forum=287&message=13863809&thread=133670&cat=9**

You can get it working with WAS Base. You can manually set different HttpSessionCloneId on Web Container custom properties on both servers, as described in:

http://publib.boulder.ibm.com/infocenter/wasinfo/v5ro//index.jsp?topic=/com.ibm.websphere.nd.doc/info/ae/ae/rprs_custom_properties.html

Quote:

Session management custom properties

You can specify additional settings for session management through setting custom properties.

To specify custom properties for session management, use the following steps:

In the administrative console click Servers > Application Servers > server_name > Web Container settings > Web Container > Custom Properties.
On the Custom Properties page, click New.
On the settings page, enter the property that you want to configure in the Name field and the value that you want to set it to in the Value field.
Click Apply or OK.
Click Save on the console task bar to save your configuration changes.
Restart the server.

CloneSeparatorChange

Use this property to maintain session affinity. The clone ID of the server is appended to session identifier separated by colon. On some Wireless Application Protocol (WAP) devices, a colon is not allowed. Set this property to "true" to change clone separator to a plus sign (+).

HttpSessionCloneId

Use this property to change the clone ID of the cluster member. Within a cluster, this name must be unique to maintain session affinity. When set, this name overwrites the default name generated by WebSphere Application Server. Default clone ID length: 8 or 9.

<u>End of Quote</u>

After that, in the new plugin-cfg.xml, for each server section there is a new property CloneID with the HttpSessionCloneId that you set for each server; also, after a WAS restart, the new JSESSIONID's generated should contain the CloneID; and now, the webserver doesn't lose its affinity.

Question 10: Virtual Host/WebGroup Not Found

We are trying to access our Webphere application. We can open the login screen, but can't login. We can't also access any page under **http://<server** name>:<port>/servlet/

When we try to access those pages, the following error is logged within WebSphere:

"PLGN0021E: Servlet Request Processor Exception: Virtual Host/WebGroup Not Found : The web group /servlet/Profile has not been defined"

We observe this problem only with 1 of the 2 applications for this server. If we use the other application's port number, everything works fine. We think the virtual host is configured correctly, and it's mapped to the right application. We have also checked the httpd.conf file and the plug-in file. We don't see any errors, and have compared these to other servers and they look identical.

It almost seems like we have a broken link or a typo somewhere. Could anyone give us his or her ideas on this problem?

```
HTTPD.CONF:
#Second Host for Test Environment
<VirtualHost *:81>

#WEBSHPERE ADDINS
WebSpherePluginConfig
C:/Websphere/AppServer/config/cells/plugin-cfg.xml

    ServerAdmin webmaster@dummy-host.example.com
    DocumentRoot
"c:/WebSphere/IBMHTTPServer2/htdocs/testenv"
    ServerName testenv.<blah>.com
    ErrorLog logs/testenv-error_log
    CustomLog logs/testenv-access_log common
ScriptAlias    /cgi-lawson/
"c:/WebSphere/IBMHTTPServer2/htdocs/testenv/cgi-
lawson/"

<Directory
c:/WebSphere/IBMHTTPServer2/htdocs/testenv/cgi-
lawson>
    AllowOverride AuthConfig
    AuthUserFIle
```

```
c:/WebSphere/IBMHTTPServer2/userdb/lawson
    AuthType Basic
    AuthName "CGI Lawson"
    Options Indexes
    Options FollowSymLinks
    Options +ExecCGI
    Require valid-user
</Directory>
<Location /servlet>
    AllowOverride AuthConfig
    AuthUserFIle
c:/WebSphere/IBMHTTPServer2/userdb/lawson
    AuthType Basic
    AuthName "CGI Lawson"
    Options Indexes
    Options FollowSymLinks
    Require valid-user
</Location>
</VirtualHost>


Plug-IN:
    <?xml version="1.0" encoding="ISO-8859-1" ?>
- <Config ASDisableNagle="false"
AcceptAllContent="false"
AppServerPortPreference="HostHeader"
ChunkedResponse="false" IISDisableNagle="false"
IISPluginPriority="High" IgnoreDNSFailures="false"
RefreshInterval="60" ResponseChunkSize="64"
VHostMatchingCompat="false">
    <Log LogLevel="Error"
Name="C:\WebSphere\AppServer/logs/http_plugin.log" />

    <Property Name="ESIEnable" Value="false" />
    <Property Name="ESIMaxCacheSize" Value="1024" />
    <Property Name="ESIInvalidationMonitor"
Value="false" />
- <VirtualHostGroup Name="test_host">
    <VirtualHost Name="*:81" />
    <VirtualHost Name="*:443" />
    </VirtualHostGroup>
- <VirtualHostGroup Name="prod_host">
    <VirtualHost Name="*:80" />
    <VirtualHost Name="*:443" />
    </VirtualHostGroup>
- <VirtualHostGroup Name="default_host">
    <VirtualHost Name="*:81" />
    <VirtualHost Name="*:80" />
    <VirtualHost Name="*:9080" />
    <VirtualHost Name="*:9443" />
    </VirtualHostGroup>
```

```
- <ServerCluster CloneSeparatorChange="false"
LoadBalance="Round Robin" Name="server1
_webserver03_Cluster" PostSizeLimit="-1"
RemoveSpecialHeaders="true" RetryInterval="60">
- <Server ConnectTimeout="0"
ExtendedHandshake="false" MaxConnections="-1"
Name="webserver03_server1" ServerIOTimeout="0"
WaitForContinue="false">
  <Transport Hostname="webserver03" Port="9080"
Protocol="http" />
- <Transport Hostname="webserver03" Port="9443"
Protocol="https">
  <Property Name="keyring"
Value="C:\WebSphere\AppServer\etc\plugin-key.kdb" />
  <Property Name="stashfile"
Value="C:\WebSphere\AppServer\etc\plugin-key.sth" />
  <Property Name="certLabel" Value="selfsigned" />
  </Transport>
  </Server>
- <PrimaryServers>
  <Server Name="webserver03_server1" />
  </PrimaryServers>
  </ServerCluster>
- <UriGroup
Name="prod_host_server1_webserver03_Cluster_URIs">
  <Uri AffinityCookie="JSESSIONID"
AffinityURLIdentifier="jsessionid" Name="*.jsp" />
  <Uri AffinityCookie="JSESSIONID"
AffinityURLIdentifier="jsessionid" Name="*.jsv" />
  <Uri AffinityCookie="JSESSIONID"
AffinityURLIdentifier="jsessionid" Name="*.jsw" />
  <Uri AffinityCookie="JSESSIONID"
AffinityURLIdentifier="jsessionid"
Name="/j_security_check" />
  <Uri AffinityCookie="JSESSIONID"
AffinityURLIdentifier="jsessionid"
Name="/ibm_security_logout" />
  <Uri AffinityCookie="JSESSIONID"
AffinityURLIdentifier="jsessionid" Name="/servlet/*"
/>
  </UriGroup>
  <Route ServerCluster="server1_webserver03_Cluster"
UriGroup="prod_host_server1_webserver03_Cluster_URIs"
VirtualHostGroup="prod_host" />
- <UriGroup
Name="default_host_server1_webserver03_Cluster_URIs">
  <Uri AffinityCookie="JSESSIONID"
AffinityURLIdentifier="jsessionid" Name="/snoop/*" />

  <Uri AffinityCookie="JSESSIONID"
AffinityURLIdentifier="jsessionid" Name="/hello" />
```

```xml
    <Uri AffinityCookie="JSESSIONID"
AffinityURLIdentifier="jsessionid" Name="/hitcount"
/>
    <Uri AffinityCookie="JSESSIONID"
AffinityURLIdentifier="jsessionid" Name="*.jsp" />
    <Uri AffinityCookie="JSESSIONID"
AffinityURLIdentifier="jsessionid" Name="*.jsv" />
    <Uri AffinityCookie="JSESSIONID"
AffinityURLIdentifier="jsessionid" Name="*.jsw" />
    <Uri AffinityCookie="JSESSIONID"
AffinityURLIdentifier="jsessionid"
Name="/j_security_check" />
    <Uri AffinityCookie="JSESSIONID"
AffinityURLIdentifier="jsessionid"
Name="/ibm_security_logout" />
    <Uri AffinityCookie="JSESSIONID"
AffinityURLIdentifier="jsessionid" Name="/servlet/*"
/>
    </UriGroup>
    <Route ServerCluster="server1_webserver03_Cluster"
UriGroup="default_host_server1_webserver03_Cluster_UR
Is" VirtualHostGroup="default_host" />
- <UriGroup
Name="test_host_server1_webserver03_Cluster_URIs">
    <Uri AffinityCookie="JSESSIONID"
AffinityURLIdentifier="jsessionid" Name="/snoop/*" />

    <Uri AffinityCookie="JSESSIONID"
AffinityURLIdentifier="jsessionid" Name="/hello" />
    <Uri AffinityCookie="JSESSIONID"
AffinityURLIdentifier="jsessionid" Name="/hitcount"
/>
    <Uri AffinityCookie="JSESSIONID"
AffinityURLIdentifier="jsessionid" Name="*.jsp" />
    <Uri AffinityCookie="JSESSIONID"
AffinityURLIdentifier="jsessionid" Name="*.jsv" />
    <Uri AffinityCookie="JSESSIONID"
AffinityURLIdentifier="jsessionid" Name="*.jsw" />
    <Uri AffinityCookie="JSESSIONID"
AffinityURLIdentifier="jsessionid"
Name="/j_security_check" />
    <Uri AffinityCookie="JSESSIONID"
AffinityURLIdentifier="jsessionid"
Name="/ibm_security_logout" />
    <Uri AffinityCookie="JSESSIONID"
AffinityURLIdentifier="jsessionid" Name="/servlet/*"
/>
    </UriGroup>
    <Route ServerCluster="server1_webserver03_Cluster"
UriGroup="test_host_server1_webserver03_Cluster_URIs"
VirtualHostGroup="test_host" />
```

```
+ <RequestMetrics armEnabled="false"
newBehavior="false" rmEnabled="false"
traceLevel="HOPS">
+ <filters enable="false" type="URI">
  <filterValues enable="false" value="/servlet/snoop"
/>
  <filterValues enable="false"
value="/webapp/examples/HitCount" />
  </filters>
- <filters enable="false" type="SOURCE_IP">
  <filterValues enable="false"
value="xxx.xxx.xxx.xxx" />
  <filterValues enable="false"
value="yyy.yyy.yyy.yyy" />
  </filters>
  </RequestMetrics>
  </Config>
```

A: Someone had a similar problem and got it done by doing the following:

1. Take a backup of your plugins-cfg.xml.
2. Then, reinstall the plug-ins.
3. In the Admin console, Environment→ virtual hosts → host alias → new, create 443;
4. Finally, stop/start the Application server.

Question 11: Migrating from tomcat to WAS

We have an application running on tomcat 4 but we need to migrate to WAS as we have installed Websphere studio.

Are there resources available for a step by step migration from tomcat to websphere?

A: For a simple web page, it is easy to deploy it on Websphere. But for creating JNDI for MySQL in websphere 6.0, you would need some help and readings. You would have to download the free book in pdf format from the IBM website -- Migrating Applications from WebLogic, JBoss and Tomcat to WebSphere V6) at **www.redbooks.ibm.com**. Other books in **www.redbooks.ibm.com** are also good.

It would take some time for you to be familiar with the interface of Websphere Application Server Developer (WSAD) Studio. But if you know eclipse, you already have an advantage in learning the studio.

Question 12: WAS IBMIHS and Virtual Hosts

We are currently testing WAS 6 - patched up to 6.0.2.5 and we are running it with IBMIHS 6, all on AIX 5.3. The application in WAS that we are using is ColdFusion MX7.

We have the pieces working okay but as we are brand new to WAS, we are having trouble understanding some of the connectivity between the three pieces. In httpd.conf, we have virtual hosts defined. We can get an index.cfm to work as expected when we have the virtual host in WAS set to *:80. In this case, all httpd defined virtual hosts process with ColdFusion but point to the root war directory, so we get the same page for example.foo.bar and test.foo.bar even though they have different roots in httpd.conf.

We can also get any one specific host to work, i.e., example.foo.bar works when set in the WAS virtual hosts area but then virtual host test.foo.bar from httpd.conf gets text output rather than being processed through ColdFusion.

So what we are having trouble understanding is how virtual hosts set up in httpd.conf interact with WAS. Is it possible to have example.foo.bar and test.foo.bar each have their own directory (within the war directory hierarchy) and still have them processed by our application (ColdFusion)?

Are there resources or insights available?

A: The Rewrite Rule is the answer to your problem.

```
<VirtualHost www3.test.foo.bar>
    ServerAdmin webadmin@foo.bar
    DocumentRoot
/www/cfusion.ear/MacromediaColdFusionMX.ear/cfusion.w
ar/www3
    ServerName www3.test.foo.bar
    ErrorLog logs/www3_error_log
    CustomLog logs/www3_access_log common
    ReWriteEngine on
    RewriteRule ^/(.*) /www3/$1 [PT]
</VirtualHost>
```

Question 13: Error creating "SOAP" connection to host "localhost"

We are new to Websphere and when we try to use wsadmin tool, we get the following error:

C:\WebSphere\AppServer\bin>wsadmin.bat -user admin -password admin
WASX7023E: Error creating "SOAP" connection to host "localhost"; exception infor
mation:
com.ibm.websphere.management.exception.ConnectorNotAvaila bleException
WASX7213I: This scripting client is not connected to a server process; please re
fer to the log file
C:\WebSphere\AppServer\logs\wsadmin.traceout for additional information.
WASX7029I: For help, enter: "$Help help"
wsadmin>

How can we fix this error?

A: Try wsadmin -conntype SOAP -port <your soap port> -username admin -password admin

Question 14: WAS 5.1.1 with jre 1.4

We have WAS 5.1, which means that by default it uses java (jre) 1.3. A colleague has mentioned that it's possible to make WAS use java 1.4 . He also recommended to use *IBM's* implementation of jre 1.4.

We've tried searching the IBM website, but we I can't seem to find the IBM 1.4 implementation or any instructions on how to integrate it with was 5.1. Could anyone kindly refer me to the relevant links?

A: You can check this link **http://www-1.ibm.com/support/docview.wss?rs=180&uid=swg2401 0272.**

Quote:

Using UpdateInstaller to apply a cumulative fix:

• Use the "Install Fix Pack" option to install your cumulative fix.

• Installing a cumulative fix uninstalls all interim fixes previously installed.

• For silent install, use the "-fixpack" option on the command line or "fixpack=true" in a response file.

Change history

• 27 April 2007: Updated Document for 5.1.1.14 SDK 1.4.2 SR7 Release

• 15 Dec 2006: Updated Document for 5.1.1.13 SDK 1.4.2 SR6 Release

• 23 June 2006: Updated Document for 5.1.1.11 SDK 1.4.2 SR5 Release

• 17 April 2006: Updated Document for 5.1.1.10 SDK 1.4.2 SR4 Release

- 16 Dec 2005: Updated Document for 5.1.1.8 SDK 1.4.2 SR3 Release

- 19 Aug 2005: Document creation

Prerequisites

Install V5.1.1 Cumulative Fix for SDKs on top of WebSphere Application Server Version 5.1.1 or 5.1.1.x.

Download the latest UpdateInstaller tool (see below in the Installation Instructions section) to install V5.1.1 Cumulative Fix 1 for Java SDKs.

End of quote.

Question 15: Version of Websphere running

Often times, our administrator installs WebSphere Portal for us, and there are instances in which I need to know the version of WebSphere Portal we are running. How can we find the version information without using the console?

A: You can check using:

#pkginfo |grep -i websphere (solaris)
#lslpp -L|grep -i websphere (aix)
#rpm -qa|grep -i websphere (linux)

Question 16: Changing context root via the WAS console

We want to change an application's console root, and we are wondering if this is possible to do in the WAS console. We are running version 5.1.

A: It may not be possible without re-deploying your application file. If you want to edit the files directly (using a text editor), you'll need to edit the application.xml files:

```
"AppServer/installedApps/{hostname}/{app}.ear/META-
INF/application.xml" AND
"AppServer/config/cells/{hostname}/applications/{app}
.ear/deployments/{app}/META-INF/application.xml".
```

Question 17: Running JUNIT code against a standalone service

We have a service built by our development team. They've tested it using JUNIT code, and started/stopped the server for each test they want to run. But this isn't appropriate for the testing that I want to do.

Is it possible for me to run the service outside of WSAD and still use the JUNIT code they've developed? Or do I have to create an application to pass my parameters to the service?

A: What you want to do is possible, unless you have very specific cache type testing needed. In that case, you may need to restart the server to have the data in cache reloaded.

The developers should create a junit test page for each service. On that page, put the input fields and a javascript to call and format the response. Then have a "master" test index page so QA can get to each test.

It takes a few minutes if you do it when you are developing the service and be sure to make that new services make QA easier. In addition, the developers should include every input field on the form. Even if it should be blank, empty, etc. QA needs to test for the unexpected so they should not limit your options. You can give these a green background but you can come up with your own scheme for the required (white), optional (pale yellow), and unentered (green).

Question 18: Updating web server plug-in

We are writing jacl script to install an application on Websphere 5, and we need to Update Web Server Plugin using wsadmin commands rather than from the console. How can we achieve it?

A: You can try using the 'exec' tcl command to call the 'GenPluginCfg.sh'.

Question 19: Wsadmin/jacl script

We are planning to write a wsadmin/jacl script to install an application. Are there available post scripts for our reference?

A: You can go to the wsadmin prompt from the bin directory of Deployment Manager.

```
wsadmin> set pluginGen [$AdminControl
completeObjectName type=PluginCfgGenerator,*]
wsadmin> $AdminControl invoke $pluginGen generate
"c:/WebSphere/DeploymentManager
c:/WebSphere/DeploymentManager/config MyServNetwork
null null plugin-cfg.xml"
```

Question 20: Resource Analyzer

Does anybody know why the WebSphere Resource Analyzer fails when Global Security is enabled on the Admin Console? If so, is there a solution?

A: Once you enable security, you must authenticate before connecting for PMI. Below is an excerpt from an IBM site:

Using PMI with security

When the WebSphere Application Server security is turned ON, the user needs to be authenticated before calling any PMI API. You can configure the %WAS_HOME%\properties\sas.client.props to choose the appropriate login source.

Question 21: com.ibm.rmi.iiop.WorkerThread problem

We are using WSAD 5.1.0 running in Windows and we have a problem with org.omg.CORBA.ORB.init (args, props);

When called from the WSAD integrated test server (5.0) running on desktop com.ibm.rmi.iiop.WorkerThread tries to run () over and over again (caught this using the profiler). It makes the JVM 100% busy and locking up the local test server).

We think that some properties file is missing but we do not know what it could be. There would be no problem if we use WSAD 5.1.1 but I can't use 5.1.1.

Running it as an application works fine. The problem comes out only when we are using it within a servlet running in the integrated nment. It does not seem to be a problem running on real Websphere server on AIX. Does anyone know of a fix for this?

A: Check out the size of the ibmorb.jar and ibmext.jar in your /appserver/java/jre/lib/ext directory. When installing some of the fix packs, it would leave you with older versions of these files. So just update these files and your problem would go away.

Question 22: session.getAttribute only works with local host URL

We successfully set a session variable at the URL http:\\localhost:9080\testWeb using the following code:

```
if (request.getParameter("openReport") != null) {
  session.setAttribute("reportName",
stringReportName);
}
```

After the session variable is set, we can then view it from any other page on my site using:
```
session.getAttribute("reportName")
```

This same code works when we use it on the URL http:\\rsc_sza:9080\testWeb (where rsc_sza is the name of my computer) but it seems to expire when we move off of the current page. We need the variable to persist throughout the entire session.

What can the problem be?

A: Try checking the session state. It sounds like the settings are off a bit. Look for the Session Manager. It is a great resource on managing session state and more.

Question 23: Websphere studio application developer

Using version 5.1.1, whenever we launch Websphere a pop up window appears asking for a directory to work from. When we bypass this window, Websphere opens up to an empty web perspective and we can't access any of our projects. How can I get this pop up window back or how can I point to a directory that contains my projects?

A: Here is what you should do: go to the DOS command prompt, C:\Program Files\IBM\WebSphere Studio\Application Developer\v5.1.1 directory, and then execute the following:

WSAPPDEV -SETWORKSPACE

Another way that you can do if you don't want to mess around on the command prompt is to create a shortcut to WSAD (wsappdev.exe) and use the -data flag. For example, the TARGET for one of our desktop shortcuts is:

"C:\Program Files\IBM\WebSphere Studio\Application Developer\v5.1.2\wsappdev.exe" -data C:\project\Tech\WSAD_work\basic_web\workspace

Question 24: DirectTalk voice response

Whenever we try to start our Voice Response, we get the following error:

"Voice Response is being started by another user. Automatic retry will be attempted in 3 minutes".

What could I do to fix this?

A: You can do one of two things:

1. Execute the "DT_shutdown" command, wait for it to finish and then try again.

Or

2. Run the "DTforce.clean" command, wait for it to finish, and then try again.

Either way, you will solve your problem, but solution no. 1 will require you to shut down the whole application to get going again.

Question 25: WSAD Debug server mode will not compile JSPs

We love WSAD 5.1.1, especially its debug server mode which allows us to step through any servlet or JSP. It was working perfectly until last week. When we try to run in debug mode we can still step through the servlet, but as soon as we call the JSP, WSAD seems to freeze and we get nothing.

We have tried uninstalling and reinstalling, but to no avail. We did get it working once but the steps were like: break the local test server configuration, WSAD prompts to fix the server, and then restart in debug mode. But since we can't remember what we did to "break" the server configuration, we can't repeat the steps. Breaking a configuration is NOT a good work-around.

So we are just wondering if someone might know what we should look at to see why debug fails to compile our JSPs. Are there some insights available on this?

A: You have to disable the "hot recompile" of the classes and the debug mode will work again. You enable/disable this option by a checkbox on the first tab of the server definition.

Question 26: Error 503: Failed to load target servlet [portal]

We have installed WebSphere Portal 5.0 in our machine. The portal worked well until when we migrated from the CloudScape database to MS SQL Server2000 database. After migrating, whenever we start the Portal Server normally, we get the error *"Error 503: Failed to load target servlet [portal]"*, which we do not get before changing the database.

The only way I can get into the portal is by adding admin on the url. We would like to be able to use the portal as before. Could anyone out there help?

A: Check if your MS SQL server is started; if not, turn it on. Once it's up, bounce your portal server and it will work. If your SQL server is up, restart it and restart portal server.

Question 27: Websphere installation

We have a 3.4GHz computer with Windows Prof with Service Pack 2. We want to learn Java and Websphere with our new computer. We have downloaded the trial copy of WebSphere Studio Application/Site Developer Version 5.1.2 and DB2 Universal Database for Windows. And we have installed Java Web start on our computer.

Do we need to install J2SE or/and J2EE? Do we need to install an Application Server? What other software do we need? What steps should we follow to successfully install Websphere and DB2?

A: The full version of WSAD (WebSphere Studio Application Developer) includes all the stuff that you need to develop in Java, especially for J2EE applications designed for Web Sphere.

To learn Java and Web Sphere, you won't need the DB2 Universal Database. You don't need a fast machine either. Memory is very important for WSAD.

Question 28: Debug Mode - Disable Step by Step

In WSAD, we run the server in debug mode 90% of the time and it works great. But every time we start the server, it switches on the "Step by Step" mode. Is there any way we can change this so starting the server in debug mode will just use my breakpoints?

A: All you have to do is to go to Preferences → WAS Debug → Uncheck 'Enable step-by-step debug mode by default'.

Question 29: Newbie with wrong Eclipse setting

We are new to JAVA programming, especially Eclipse. We have a small program that runs fine outside of Eclipse. However, when we run it from within Eclipse, we get this error:

java.lang.NoClassDefFoundError: org/apache/log4j/Logger
    at java.lang.ClassLoader.defineClass0(Native Method)
    at java.lang.ClassLoader.defineClass(Unknown Source)
    at java.security.SecureClassLoader.defineClass(Unknown
Source)
    at java.net.URLClassLoader.defineClass(Unknown Source)
    at java.net.URLClassLoader.access$100(Unknown Source)
    at java.net.URLClassLoader$1.run(Unknown Source)
    at java.security.AccessController.doPrivileged(Native Method)
    at java.net.URLClassLoader.findClass(Unknown Source)
    at java.lang.ClassLoader.loadClass(Unknown Source)
    at sun.misc.Launcher$AppClassLoader.loadClass(Unknown
Source)
    at java.lang.ClassLoader.loadClass(Unknown Source)
    at java.lang.ClassLoader.loadClassInternal(Unknown Source)
    at com.ncr.teradata.jdbc_4.Driver.<clinit>(Unknown Source)
    at
com.ncr.teradata.jdbc_3.ifjdbc_4.TeraLocalConnection.<init>(
Unknown Source)
    at com.ncr.teradata.TeraDriver.connect(Unknown Source)
    at java.sql.DriverManager.getConnection(Unknown Source)
    at java.sql.DriverManager.getConnection(Unknown Source)
    at MyFirstApp.main(MyFirstApp.java:44)
Exception in thread "main"

The code for line 44 is:
```
con = DriverManager.getConnection(url_type4,
username, passwd);
```

If we go to a command prompt, we can likewise run the program fine. But it won't just run from within Eclipse. What do we need to change to get it to run properly?

A: You need to put the log4J jar in your classpath. To do it inside of WebSphere Studio Application Developer, this is built on top of eclipse. You need to right click on the package you are working with and click properties. Look for the area that has 'Java Build Path' and click 'Add Jars'. You can find the jar in the directory where you installed java.

Question 30: Detailed instructional material for websphere

We would like to ask where a "detailed step by step instructional materials" for websphere can be found or downloaded. We are interested in learning jsp and servlets with websphere and unfortunately, the resources which we find is either lacking in detail. They assume that you already know or they won't offer any instruction at all. Is there a resource available? Is there a good link or URL available?

A: You can refer from:
http://publib.boulder.ibm.com/infocenter/wasinfo/i.

This URL points to most of the documentation that IBM has. As for learning JSP and servlets, you need a separate java J2EE book.

Question 31: Automating installation

Is there anyway to automate the installation of the Websphere Application server program? Is there any command line arguments or configuration files that we can use? We would like to create packages for our software wherever possible so that our server installations are all identical.

Is this possible at all?

A: You can setup a response file that the installer will read instead of prompting you with questions. The file is named responsefile in the operating-system platform directory on the cd. This only relates to WAS5.x

Question 32: JavaBean -> PCML -> RPG

We are wondering whether anyone has tried using this method before to retrieve or call the legacy system that was coded in RPG. We are having some problem where our IBM WebSphere Application Server couldn't locate our PCML files although we have put that file in our CLASSPATH.

A: You could get it working from within the WDSc. The pcml file has to reside in the same location as the class file. Also, if this class file is in a package, then the PCML file name has to be prefixed with that package. Below is an example code:

CODE

```
    public static double lookup(AS400 as400, String
customer, String branch, String product) throws
PcmlException {
        double price = 0.0;

        // Create Data Objects
        ProgramCallDocument pcml;                    //
com.ibm.as400.data.ProgramCallDocument
        boolean rc = false;                          //
Return code for program call
        String msgId, msgText;                       //
Messages returned from AS/400

        // Instantiate the Objects (assign the
variables)
        pcml = new ProgramCallDocument(as400,
"com.ejiw.mincron.hd.PricingLookup");
        pcml.setValue("program.cust", customer);
        pcml.setValue("program.brch", branch);
        pcml.setValue("program.prod", product);

        // Debug statement...Use to view outbound and
inbound parms if you need it
        //com.ibm.as400.data.PcmlMessageLog.setTraceE
nabled(true);

        // Call the Program
        System.out.println("Calling JVCPRICE...");
        rc = pcml.callProgram("program");

        // If return code is false, get messages from
the iSeries
        if(rc == false) {
            // Retrieve list of AS/400 messages
            AS400Message[] msgs =
```

```
pcml.getMessageList("program");

            // Loop through all messages and write
them to standard output
            for (int m = 0; m < msgs.length; m++)
            {
                msgId = msgs[m].getID();
                msgText = msgs[m].getText();
                System.out.println("     " + msgId + "
- " + msgText);
            }
            System.out.println("Call to PROGRAM
failed. See messages listed above");
        }
        else { // Return code was true, call to
PROGRAM succeeded - woo-hoo!
            BigDecimal prc =
(BigDecimal)pcml.getValue("program.price");
            price = prc.doubleValue();
        }

        return price;
    }
```

CODE

```
<pcml version="4.0">
    <program name="program"
path="/QSYS.LIB/TESTJM.LIB/JVCPRICE.PGM"
threadsafe="false">
        <data name="cust" length="6" type="char"
usage="input" />
        <data name="brch" length="3" type="char"
usage="input" />
        <data name="prod" length="12" type="char"
usage="input" />
        <data name="price" length="7" precision="2"
type="packed" usage="output"/>
    </program>
</pcml>
```

Question 33: Installing DeploymentManager Server without an appserver server1

We would like to install a Deployment (5.1) Manager version of WebSphere and an application server on a single system. We use the silent install and everything goes fine as long as we create a server1. But we would like to have no server one and just run an AddNode.sh and create a new server using the DeploymentManager. We get all kinds of Corba-JNDI lookup errors.

Has anyone tried this before? Are there available references on this?

A: You need to have server1 to keep your administration application / jvm in it. Thus, server1 is necessary. Later on, you may create cluster and add the nodes from other servers.

Question 34: PCML Exception

I am new to PCML and went through the wizard to create the Program Call Beans. Then I created the below method to run the RPG program. When I ran it though, I got the following exception. Does anyone have any idea on how to fix this?

CODE

```
    public static void lookup(int cnum) {

        try {
            AS400JDBCDriver driver = new
AS400JDBCDriver();
            AS400 as400 = new AS400(sysname,
username, password);
            driver.connect(as400);

            CustLookup look = new CustLookup();
            look.setCnum(new Integer(cnum));
            look.setCname("");
            look.setConnectionData(as400);
            look.invoke();
            System.out.println("Customer  " +
look.getCnum() + " - " + look.getCname());

        }
        catch(Exception e) {
            System.out.println(e.getMessage() + "\n"
+ e.toString());
            e.printStackTrace();
        }

    }
```

DE

```
_____Thread 0 = main
304529:47:28.851 0 > Unable to create
ProgramCallDocument :
com.ibm.as400.data.PcmlException: Text not available
for error message key
'java.util.MissingResourceException'
 Error in processing ProgramCall project :
ProjectName = [CustLookup]

com.ibm.connector.LogonException:  Error in
processing ProgramCall project : ProjectName =
[CustLookup]

com.ibm.connector.LogonException:  Error in
processing ProgramCall project : ProjectName =
```

```
[CustLookup]
        at
com.ibm.connector.as400.AS400LogonLogoff.logon(AS400L
ogonLogoff.java:302)
        at
com.ibm.connector.as400.AS400Connection.logon(AS400Co
nnection.java:247)
        at
com.ibm.connector.as400.AS400Connection.open(AS400Con
nection.java:283)
        at
com.ibm.connector.as400.AS400Communication.connect(AS
400Communication.java:132)
        at
com.ibm.ivj.eab.command.CommandCommunicationPrimitive
.oldBeforeExecute(CommandCommunicationPrimitive.java:
638)
        at
com.ibm.ivj.eab.command.CommandCommunicationPrimitive
.beforeExecute(CommandCommunicationPrimitive.java:95)
        at
com.ibm.ivj.eab.command.CommunicationCommand.connEtoM
1(CommunicationCommand.java:222)
        at
com.ibm.ivj.eab.command.CommunicationCommand.beforeIn
ternalExecution(CommunicationCommand.java:102)
        at
com.ibm.connector.as400.ProgramCallCommand.beforeInte
rnalExecution(ProgramCallCommand.java:592)
        at
com.ibm.ivj.eab.command.Command.fireBeforeInternalExe
cution(Command.java:363)
        at
com.ibm.ivj.eab.command.Command.execute(Command.java:
283)
        at
com.ibm.ivj.eab.command.Command.execute(Command.java:
254)
        at
com.ibm.ivj.eab.command.CommunicationCommand.execute(
CommunicationCommand.java:671)
        at
com.ibm.iseries.webint.WebIntProgramCall.execute(WebI
ntProgramCall.java:395)
        at
com.ibm.connector.as400.ProgramCallBean.invoke(Progra
mCallBean.java:121)
        at
com.ejiw.test.CustLookup.invoke(CustLookup.java:47)
        at
```

```
com.ejiw.test.CustomerLookup.lookup(CustomerLookup.ja
va:19)
     at
com.ejiw.test.CustomerLookup.main(CustomerLookup.java
:37)
```

A: The error means that it can't locate the PCML file. This file needs to reside in the same spot as the class file. The wizards sometimes grossly over-complicate the process. You may want to just key in PCML file and Java program manually as it is much simpler.

Question 35: Websphere application server help

I own a copy of <u>websphere</u> application server 3.02. Aside from its website development capabilities, I am not sure what it does. The IBM website refers to e business solutions but does not specify. Where can I get some tangible examples of this software's prowess? Could anyone give me a link to a reference?

A: First of all, it is no longer recommended to use version 3.0.2. It is quite old and it might have reached its end of service date. The business aspect they are referring to probably has to do with what the J2EE spec handles today. Look on Sun's <u>website</u> for the latest spec.

<u>IBM</u> has stopped supporting this version of websphere. What websphere can do also varies on which edition you have. But to continue getting the best out of Websphere 3, you need to upgrade it to version 3.5.

Question 36: Wsadmin - JVM custom properties

Does anyone know how to set a JVM custom property in wsadmin? I know how to do it through Web Console (Application Servers → myServer → Process Definition → Java Virtual Machine → Custom Properties) but would much prefer to script this.

Any advice I can use?

A: To be able to do what you prefer, do the following:
CODE
```
set as [$AdminConfig getid
/Cell:$cellName/Node:$nodeName/Server:$appServerName/
]

    # IBM Service Activity Log
    set rls [$AdminConfig list RASLoggingService $as]
    $AdminConfig modify $rls [subst {{serviceLog
{{enabled true} {name $activitylog} {size 2}}}}]

    # IBM Diagnostic Trace Service Log
    set ts [$AdminConfig list TraceService $as]
    $AdminConfig modify $ts [subst {{traceLog
{{fileName $tracelog} {maxNumberOfBackupFiles 1}
{rolloverSize 20}}}}]

    $AdminConfig save
```

Question 37: StaleConnection exception on WAS 4.x

We get the following exception after our <u>database</u> does an incremental backup daily every time. After the backup, the first hit to the database is throwing the StaleConnection exception. But then afterwards, it works just fine till the next scheduled backup. We believe the backup process shuts down all the database connections to run. Does anyone have any suggestion?

A: Your problem just means that the DB connectivity disappears during backup and that your connection pool has some connections that are no longer valid. As your application gets connection from the pool, these will be replaced with valid connections. If it bothers you, it might worth doing <u>online backup</u>.

Question 38: WebSphere administrator

I am new to Websphere and we are evaluating <u>websphere</u> administrators. Could anyone give us insights with the type of questions that would help us to quantify and qualify candidates?

A: Extensive knowledge of J2EE is a must. Also, knowledge in wsadmin jacl <u>scripting</u> would be beneficial. Jacl is useful, but mostly if the Admin wants to use it. You may not put too much emphasis on jacl ability, unless you are looking to automate a lot of your administration tasks. If the potential admin brings up scripting and other administration automation objectives, then it shows ability a step above the rest. A deep understanding of basic J2EE is very important, as is a deep understanding of <u>IBM</u> help systems. You need an admin that knows how to figure things out without the manual as they will run into situations they have never seen before, and IBM has probably never seen before.

Question 39: WebSphere Error: Failed Initialization

I just finished installing Websphere on an AIX machine (version 5). Installation went fine but when I start the server, it gives the message: "Server Launched but failed initialization". When I verify the installation, I get many error messages saying:

Server server1 failed to start
Error occurred during setup
Failed to start transport on host, port 9090.
The most likely cause is the port is already in use.

I know for a fact that I am the only one on this server and that there is no way this port is in use.

What could be wrong?

A: Websphere conflicts with wsm. The best way that you could do is to disable the wsmserver port 9090 in /etc/services and reboot.

Question 40: WebSphere global security breaks admin console

I have been enabling global security on all my WAS 5.0 environments using the same process. However, on one of my servers when I enable it, I get an "error 500" message when I try and access the admin console application. All the other applications work correctly. If I disable it then the admin console works fine. I know that my user repository is setup correctly as I have to use the correct password to use the wsadmin tool. The only suspicious errors I could find in the logs are the following:

```
[1/14/04 16:40:31:696 CST] 614acc33 WebGroup E
SRVE0026E:[Servlet Error]-[]:
java.lang.NullPointerException at
com.ibm.ejs.models.base.bindings.applicationbnd.impl.
SubjectImpl.hashCode(SubjectImpl.java:83)
...
...
[1/14/04 16:40:32:763 CST] 614acc33 WebGroup I
SRVE0180I:[adminconsole] [/admin] [Servlet.LOG]:
/error.jsp: init
[1/14/04 16:40:41:596 CST] 43ed8c30 OSEListenerDi E
PLGN0021E: Servlet Request Processor Exception:
Virtual Host/WebGroup Not Found : The web group / has
not been defined
```

A: Basically, the problem is caused by invalid console users or console groups. You just have to go into the admin console, and under system administration, delete the users and groups. After that, you can re-enable security. For further readings on this, go to the IBM's developer zone website.

Question 41: IBM WS AdminServer 4.0 service terminated with service-specific error

I have installed <u>WebSphere</u> 4.0.4 on a Windows 2000 Server, but when I try to start the AdminServer I get the following error message:

"Windows could not start the <u>IBM</u> WS AdminServer 4.0 on Local Computer. For more information, review the System event log. If this is a non-Microsoft service, contact the service vendor, and refer to service-specific error code 10."

When I check the event viewer, it says that the "IBM WS AdminServer 4.0 service was terminated with service-specific error 10." Could anyone help?

A: You must reinstall the WAS, using the step by step installation from IBM Websphere V4.0 advanced edition. You can download it from the redbooks.

Question 42: IBM Websphere & IIS

1. We are in the process of deploying our application on IBM Websphere 5.0 with IIS set up, which is installed on a remote machine. Is there any way to ensure that plug-in is configured for IIS properly?

2. We tried giving the URL as **http://www.a.com:9080/snoop** and it works fine. This means that the embedded HTTP server is working fine.

3. We tried giving the URL as **http://www.a.com:80/snoop** and it is giving "Page not found" error. This means that the IIS is not working fine. But we can see the IIS service ON, listening on port 80. What may be the reason?

4. We have created a war and deployed it. In this war, just for testing purpose, we have created one servlet that does not access DB and another servlet that accesses DB. The servlet without DB- related stuff is working fine and the one with DB related tasks is not working fine. We have created the appropriate data source. What does this imply?

We found that both the IIS and the embedded HTTP servers are working fine individually. Now, the only thing that can be suspected is "Plug In". Can any one tell us how to configure the generated Plug-In file for IIS? Both IIS and Websphere application server are installed on the same machine. Could anyone give us hints about this problem?

A: If you have IIS and WebSphere being deployed on the same server, you just need to install the plug in for IIS from the WebSphere application server CD. Some encountered problems with installing IIS on a remote machine from WebSphere, but installing IIS on the same machine is not a problem. Just simply stop the IBM http server from running and then install the plug in for IIS using the CD, and then through WebSphere admin console, regenerate the plug in and it would work fine.

Question 43: Installing mqseries 5.3 on windows XP

We are moving from win2000 to winXP. When we try to install mqs 5.3 from the IBM CDROM, we get the following message:

< this platform is not taken in consideration for this websphere MQ version but it will be in the next CSD>

What's the problem? Has somebody encountered this? Is there a solution?

A: You need version 5.3.1 for XP. The initial release didn't support XP at that stage.

Question 44: Learning websphere

Can Webspere run on windows or does it perform best on linux. Also, can a demo copy of this software be obtained? Can somebody recommend books for websphere beginners?

A: Yes, Websphere can be run on Windows. IBM also has a 60-day trial version of Websphere that you can download directly from the IBM. Below are some books which you may use to familiarize yourself with Websphere:

http://publib-b.boulder.ibm.com/cgi-bin/searchsite.cgi?...
http://www.wiley.com/WileyCDA/WileyTitle/productCd-0471...
http://www.wiley.com/WileyCDA/WileyTitle/productCd-0471...

For administration books, you may visit this link:

http://publib-b.boulder.ibm.com/cgi-bin/searchsite.cgi?...

Question 45: Plug-in development in WebSphere

I am trying to develop a <u>plug in</u> for WSAD. I want the plug in to be another perspective in WSAD. I have created a plug in with the plug in wizard using the Plug-in with perspective extensions. But when I run the plug in project, no perspective comes up. Could somebody help and explain this?

A: It seems you need some more readings on Websphere. You should check **www.eclipse.org**
and you will find there useful articles and <u>tutorials</u> about this.

Question 46: Websphere 4 XMLConfig import problems

I am in the beginning stages of writing some scripts to update the Application server properties in WebSphere. I have a lot of JVM arguments to add and as new ones come down the pipe, I plan on the following:

1) Do a partial export of the application server(s) with XMLConfig.

2) Manually edit the exported xml with the new properties added.

3) Use XMLConfig - import to re-import the application server configuration with the new (additional) properties.

I haven't gotten past my first test run. I can do a partial export of one particular application server, but when I take the xml file that the export creates and try to re-import it (without any mods at all) XMLConfig throws the following message:

FatalError: On line 1, Column: 6,037
Message: Character reference "" is an invalid XML character.
XMLC0139W: You may be using an incompatible XML config file.

Since this is an xml file and XMLConfig generated, I would think it would be a compatible file to import as well. The bottom line question is: How do I get around this problem to re-import partially exported xml? Also, here's what the first two lines of the partially exported xml looks like.

<?xml version="1.0"?>
<!DOCTYPE websphere-sa-config SYSTEM
"file:///$XMLConfigDTDLocation$$dsep$xmlconfig.dtd" >

What are these errors about?

A: The error is caused by the DTD not being referenced correctly. If you change the DTD reference line to the actual location of your DTD, then it would work. Also, try to export from the AdminConsole GUI.

Check your characters. Sometimes, some weird combination of characters in the JVM arguments acts as a control character. Just remove it if you don't need that property anyway.

The "" character in the error message is a blank space. Remove it.

Question 47: IBM HTTP Server talking to a WebSphere machine on AIX

I have a Windows 2000 machine running IBM HTTP Server 1.3.26. I need it to access and communicate with WebSphere on an AIX box (Both version 5) and I need to do it via a browser. I have been trying to do it by typing the browser:

http://<name of windows machine/<AIXMachine>:9080/PlantsByWebSphere/

I get 'forbidden access' when I do this. Can anyone give me some insight into this?

A: First, let us assume that both the HTTP Server and WebSphere are running on the Windows machine. The log files for WebSphere are under WEBSPHERE_ROOT/logs. Go and look for the tracefile and any files that have *stderr* and *stdout* in the file name. The tracefile is most useful on startup of WebSphere and the other files will log info on a running basis. There will always be a *stderr* and *stdout* file for each servlet that is running on your server.

Now, as far as your error is concerned in accessing your application, try the IP address or hostname of the webserver machine followed by the port name, then the location of the servlet Plants... For example: **http://192.168.1.1:80/PlantsByWebSphere**. You need to know the IP address and port number of the web server and also the location of the app which it seems is Plants.

Assuming again that you started WebSphere on the AIX box with startupServer.sh, you can start the administration client for WebSphere by typing adminclient.sh. Both are in the /usr/WebSphere/AppServer/bin.

You can test WebSphere by typing (if the servlet snoop is running) **http://appserver_name/servlet/snoop** where the appserver_name is the name of the machine running WebSphere.

Bottom line, your problem is that you just have too many servers in your original URL.

Question 48: Getting the list of channels

We are trying to get a list of all channels known to the local queue manager. The idea is to display their name and status. But I am not too sure how to go about this. I need a solution/hint based around C code.

A: Below are some quotes which you may to read to understand your problem.

Inquiring about queue attributes using MQINQ

Attributes are the properties that define the characteristics of an MQSeries object, including queues. They affect the way the object is handled by the queue manager. Some attributes are set when the object is initially defined, and can only be changed via MQSeries commands.

An application can inquire about all the queue attributes using the MQINQ call. The MQI also provides the MQSET call (outlined later) in order to allow applications to change some of the queue attributes. The MQINQ call uses an array of selectors to identify those attributes whose current values are to be inquired about. There is a selector for each of the attributes an application can work with. Before an application can use MQINQ it must first have been connected to the queue manager using MQCONN and have opened a queue for inquiry using MQOPEN.

Input to the MQINQ

* A connection handle returned from a previous MQCONN call
* The queue object handle returned a previous MQOPEN call for the desired queue
* The number of selectors in the attribute selector array
* An array of attribute selectors whose values are set via the MQSeries named constants. Each selector represents an attribute whose current value is to be inquired about. Selectors can be specified in any order in the array
* The number of integer type attributes to be inquired about. Specify zero if no integer type attributes are specified in the selectors array
* The address of an integer array with enough elements to hold the output integer attribute values
* The length of the character attributes buffer. This must be at least the sum of the lengths required to hold each character

attribute string being inquired about. Specify zero if no character
type attributes are inquired about
* The address of the character buffer to hold the returned
attribute values

Output from MQINQ

* A completion code
* A reason code
* A set of integer attribute values copied into the specified integer
array
* The buffer in which character attribute values have been copied

Question 49: Publishing web services problem

I am trying to publish a simple web service using IBM's Public UDDI Test Registry. I have developed a web service which I tested using the sample generated within Websphere Application Developer and it works perfectly. Once I tested the web service, I published the business entity and published the service with the uddi test registry but the URL I am using for the WSDL file must be incorrect. I am publishing the web service by launching the UDDI explorer from within Websphere Application Developer.

I was able to publish the web service but when I import the WSDL to another web project and attempt to use it, I receive an error. I imported the wsdl file and generated a web service client. I then used the sample generated (TestClient.jsp) but the following error occurs:

Exception: [SOAPException: faultCode=SOAP-ENV:Protocol; msg=Unsupported response content type "text/html", must be: "text/xml".
Response was: Virtual Host or Web Application Not Found
The web group /WSWEB/servlet/rpcrouter has not been defined
IBM WebSphere Application Server]

The link (/WSWEB/servlet/rpcrouter) to the rpcrouter from the error above is pointing to the rpcrouter from the web project I used to create the web service originally and export the WSDL. Any ideas on what the problem is or could anyone point me to a good tutorial, although I have looked and followed most of the tutorials I could find related to web services in developer works.

How can I resolve this?

A: Check your configuration setting as you may be missing something. Go to Window → Preferences → Internet and then click on "enable proxy server". Rerun your service.

Question 50: Problem in installation on AIX and Solaris

I installed WAS 5.0 for a client on AIX box, but when I try to install fix packs 5.01, I get the following error: *"can't find libjava.a file"*. What's wrong with this?

I installed WAS 5.0 for another client on Solaris box, then I installed fix packs 5.01 easily. But when I install fix packs 5.02, I get the error *"JAVA_HOME is not set up"*. I did run setupClient.sh and setupCmdLine.sh before running updateWizard.sh.

What can I do to fix this?

A: To install fixpack1, you must run setupCmdLine.sh like this:
root@server> . /webpsherePAth/bin/setupCmdLine.sh

The "." specifies that the variables in the setupCmdLine will be exported to the current shell environment.

Question 51: WAS 5.0 does not recompile JSP files

After updating from WAS 4.0.2 to WAS 5.0.2, the new WAS compiles any JSP files only once. All further changes to a JSP file are ignored - "reloading" a JSP-page inside the browser results everytime in the same (old) output. By only stopping and restarting the appropriate AppServer makes WAS recompile the JSP, but only once again. It looks like a caching problem to me but
* browser cache is disabled / browser configured probably
* no proxy server is involved
* dynamic caching inside WAS is disabled
* servlet caching inside WAS is disabled
* ESI caching inside plugin-cfg.xml is disabled
* making the WAR-module "reloadable" (every 3 seconds) doesn't help
* even deleting the .class files from the /temp/... directory doesn't help
* and deleting the JSP from the server!!! doesn't work as well - the (old) output is still returned, although the file no longer exists.

Load balancing via edge components load balancer is used but I don't think the problem is related to the balancer (CachingProxy is not used).

Does anybody know, what WAS 5.0.2 is doing? WAS 4.0.2 realized any changes to the JSP-source code without problems. Why doesn't it work with WAS 5.0? Can ClassLoaders be involved in this mystery?

A: The key to your problem is the "hot deployment"-related setting for dynamic class reloading. Unfortunately, the appropriate setting for this is located in three different XML-configuration files (one for the WAR, one for the EAR, and one for the APP-Server itself) and each of the file is being overruled by the next file resulting in the APP-Server XML-configuration file being the sole "master configuration" file.

Your fault may be that (a) only one of the configuration files had the appropriate changes for dynamic class-reloading, while the other files didn't. Thus they overruled your settings. (b) When changing to the APP-Server configuration, additional settings have to be done in WAS 5.x in order to make this "master-configuration" takes effect. You must not miss these additional steps.

The key to solving this problem is "hot deployment" and "dynamic class reloading". Check any available documentation files / PDF's for these terms to get an idea which settings are required.

Question 52: encountering WorkRolledbackException

I am using websphere 4.0 when getting a connection from the DataSource and do a SELECT statement. But whenever I close the connection, it throws an exception message below:

"WorkRolledbackException: Outstanding work on this connection was not committed or rolled back by the user and has been rolledback."

I did not change anything. I just selected a few rows, select * from mytable. I don't want to rollback every time I use the DB although I read on the net that I can do that to avoid this exception. I don't encounter this problem if i use DriverManager.getConnection() but I want to use DataSources.

What can I do to fix this?

A: According to IBM, WebSphere will throw this exception if setAutoCommit(false) is set on the connection and there is no explicit commit/rollback prior to the connection being closed. You have three options to avoid the exception:

1. Don't use setAutoCommit(false) -- at least not on selects
2. Explicitly call commit or rollback prior to closing the connection, and
3. Wrap your close statement in a try/catch and do nothing in the catch.

Question 53: SSL Configuration Problem

I face a big problem every time I try to configure the SSL for my Websphere Application Server. I have enabled the SSL with Dummy Keys (Websphere Built-in). When I try to access my application from the browser, it gives the message

unexpected message; perhaps the server's SSL security level is higher than the client can perform

and on the browser, it shows three whit boxes (three control characters)

I have updated my IE Encryption level to 128 bit.

What can I do to fix this?

A: After configuring SSL in WebSphere Application Server (WAS) AE 4.0.1 (not in the web server), the following exception may occur when starting restarting WAS: *unexpected message; perhaps the server's SSL security level is higher than the client can perform*. This may occur for the following reasons:

1. The certificates may not contain all the information they need. Ensure that in addition to the main certificate, the signer certificate is also added to the certificate database file.
2. The certificate label being imported into the certificate database file may contain spaces. Remove all spaces from the certificate label.
3. There may be a mismatch between the encryption algorithms used between the client and server. This most likely would occur if configuring SSL between the plug in and WAS, and the two are on separate machines. Make sure the algorithms supported by the security level set in WAS is also configured on the plug in box too.

Question 54: WebSphere 5 Embedded Messaging

Could anybody explain why I receive the message *"WebSphere Embedded Messaging has not been installed"* during start up? I don't understand how embedded messaging may not be installed. I'm using WebSphere 5 Trial and it is a full installation.

I created JmsTopicConnectionFactory through adminconsole and bind application local resource
to this factory installing this ear to server. But when I try to look up local resource, I get NameNotFoundException for this factory.

A: IBMwas5_trial_for_nt.zip does not contain Embedded Messaging. Download messaging_trial_for_nt.zip, merged them and then reinstall WebSphere.

Question 55: Two versions of WAS on the same machine

Is it possible to execute two different versions (3.5 and 4.0) of Websphere on the same machine?
Is there a compatibility table that exists of all these versions?

What can I do to fix this?

A: Yes, you can have multiple versions of WAS on the same server. It is possible even with multiple instances of the same version allowing for different fixpack levels. Just keep the paths different and the ports separated in the admin.config and have each version's entry of "LoadModule ibm_app_server_http_module <path_to_object>/mod_ibm_app_server_http.so" in the active httpd.conf file.

Check this out for more information:

http://www-3.ibm.com/software/webservers/appserv/doc/v40/ae/infocenter/was/rncoexist.html

Question 56: Deployment Files in Websphere App developer

Whenever I make a bean and generate the deployment files in Webshpere Studio Application Developer, it creates many additional files in my project folder. I am assuming these are all related to the deployment of the beans to the integrated Websphere server. For example: EJSStatelessTestSessionHomeBean_cb635b97.java

Does anyone know if these should be packaged up with the EAR or are they unnecessary for deployment to a standalone Websphere server? I am somewhat confused as to what to do with them.

What can I do to fix this?

A: WebSphere Studio Application Developer generates deployment artifacts it needs in the EAR file and you should not concern yourself with these if you have used the normal project folder structure. The Studio will use them to construct the EAR file. The basic rule of thumb is this – let Studio manage these resources unless you absolutely have to override its folder assignments.

Question 57: IBM wsdk v5 running appserver command errors

I found that in the file "*appserver/bin/setWSDKProperties.sh*", all the if-statements are in the form of: if [[...]] and it produces error messages like: ......sh: [[: command not found when I run the command "appserver start", or "appserver list", "appserver stop", etc.

Since most of the application server command would call this file, they all have such problems. Does anyone else encounter this problem? Do I need to modify them myself?

What can I do to fix this?

A: It looks like you have not given the <servername> in the command. Have you looked at the Administration Model sections of the Info Center? These are .jacl scripts you are running underneath the shell commands and the errors you are getting look like they're from the wsadmin Jacl interpreter. You should be able to find examples in the InfoCenter, search for 'startServer'.

Question 58: Websphere Server Set-up

Should Websphere be set up on a separate box from db2? The box I have it set up on includes db2. This sometimes causes problems with Websphere, either slowing it down or stopping it if there are problems writing to the database.

What can I do to fix this?

A: WebSphere and DB2 can be on the same box. But you have to make sure that your box can handle both. It's probably slowing down/stopping because of the resources. Another culprit could be the connections you have set for DB2 and WAS or even the sql statements you have defined. So check it out also.

Question 59: Too many open files

The application I'm working with works on WSAD V4 but not on V5. I'm getting too many open files error. This occurs when doing multiple file transformations (XSD/XSLT). Some of the XSD files being transformed have multiple imports. The number of XSD files transformed is around 350 files. Is there a way to close Files, or StreamSource's? I've set them to null after the transform, but that doesn't seem to help. Also, when this happens I have to restart WSAD. It's strange that this does not occur on Version 4 (I am using the Version 4 Test Server in WSAD 5).

code:
```
Source xslSource = new StreamSource(stylesheet);
TransformerFactory transFact =
TransformerFactory.newInstance();
Templates templates =
transFact.newTemplates(xslSource);

for (int i=0; i<msgs.length; i++)
{
   File htmFile = new File(toPath, msgs + "_v" +
version + ".htm");
   File xsdFile = new File(msgPath, msgs + ".xsd");

   if (!htmFile.exists())
   {
      StreamSource sourceXSD = new
StreamSource(xsdFile);
      StreamResult resultHTM = new
StreamResult(htmFile);
      Transformer trans =
templates.newTransformer();
      trans.setParameter("docpath",
msgPath.getAbsolutePath() +
         System.getProperty("file.separator"));

      trans.transform(sourceXSD,
resultHTM);   <---------------FAILS HERE
      xsdFile = null;
      htmFile = null;
      sourceXSD = null;
      resultHTM = null;
   }
}

File[] docs = toPath.listFiles();
```

```
BatchDistributionUtil.zipFiles(docs, new File(toPath,
"documentation.zip"));

*** Starting the server ***
IBM WebSphere Application Server, Release 4.0.4
Advanced Single Server Edition for Multiplatforms
Copyright IBM Corp., 1997-2001

************ Start Display Current Environment
************
WebSphere AEs 4.0.4 ptf40230.02 running with process
name
localhost/Default Server and process id 1504
Host Operating System is Windows 2000, version 5.0
Java version = J2RE 1.3.1 IBM Windows 32 build
cn131w-20020710 ORB130
(JIT enabled: jitc), Java Compiler = jitc, Java VM
name = Classic VM
server.root = D:\Program Files\IBM\WebSphere
Studio\runtimes\aes_v4
Java Home = D:\Program Files\IBM\WebSphere
Studio\runtimes\aes_v4\java\jre
ws.ext.dirs = D:\Program Files\IBM\WebSphere
Studio\runtimes\aes_v4/java/lib;D:\Program
Files\IBM\WebSphere
Studio\runtimes\aes_v4/classes;D:\Program
Files\IBM\WebSphere
Studio\runtimes\aes_v4/lib;D:\Program
Files\IBM\WebSphere
Studio\runtimes\aes_v4/lib/ext;D:\Program
Files\IBM\WebSphere
Studio\runtimes\aes_v4/web/help;D:/Program
Files/IBM/WebSphere
Studio/wstools/eclipse/plugins/com.ibm.etools.websphe
re.tools.common_5.0.2/runtime/wasListener.jar;D:/Prog
ram
Files/IBM/WebSphere
Studio/wstools/eclipse/plugins/com.ibm.etools.webserv
ice_5.0.2/runtime/worf.jar
Classpath = D:\Program Files\IBM\WebSphere
Studio\runtimes\aes_v4/properties;D:\Program
Files\IBM\WebSphere
Studio\runtimes\aes_v4/lib/bootstrap.jar;D:/Program
Files/IBM/WebSphere
Studio/wstools/eclipse/plugins/com.ibm.etools.websphe
re.tools.common_5.0.2/runtime/wteServers.jar;D:/Progr
am
Files/IBM/WebSphere
Studio/wstools/eclipse/plugins/com.ibm.etools.websphe
re.tools.common_5.0.2/runtime/wasToolsCommon.jar
Java Library path = D:\Program Files\IBM\WebSphere
```

```
Studio\runtimes\aes_v4/bin;D:\Program
Files\IBM\WebSphere
Studio\eclipse\jre\bin;.;C:\WINNT\System32;C:\WINNT;D
:\Program
Files\IBM\WebSphere
Studio\runtimes\base_v5\bin;D:\Program
Files\IBM\WebSphere MQ\Java\bin;D:/Program
Files/IBM/WebSphere
MQ/WEMPS\bin;D:\Program Files\IBM\WebSphere
MQ\Java\lib;D:\oracle\ora81\bin;C:\Program
Files\Oracle\jre\1.1.7\bin;C:\WINNT\system32;C:\WINNT
;C:\WINNT\System32\Wbem;D:\Program
Files\Hummingbird\Connectivity\7.00\Accessories\;d:\P
rogram
Files\Rational\ClearQuest;d:\unixtools;D:\Program
Files\IBM\WebSphere
MQ\bin;D:\Program Files\IBM\WebSphere
MQ\WEMPS\bin;C:\jdk1.3.1_02\bin;C:\Tools\Ant\bin;C:\P
rogram
Files\Microsoft Visual Studio\Common\VSS\win32
Current trace specification = *=all=disabled
************ End Display Current Environment
*************
[5/14/03 10:32:51:750 EDT] 67195e54 Server          U
Version : 4.0.4
[5/14/03 10:32:51:766 EDT] 67195e54 Server          U
Edition: Advanced
Single Server Edition for Multiplatforms
[5/14/03 10:32:51:766 EDT] 67195e54 Server          U
Build date: Thu
Sep 05 00:00:00 EDT 2002
[5/14/03 10:32:51:766 EDT] 67195e54 Server          U
Build number:
ptf40230.02
[5/14/03 10:32:54:391 EDT] 67195e54 DrAdminServer I
WSVR0053I: DrAdmin
available on port 7000
[5/14/03 10:32:54:516 EDT] 67195e54 ResourceBinde I
WSVR0049I: Binding
Session Persistence datasource as jdbc/Session
[5/14/03 10:32:55:922 EDT] 67195e54 ServletEngine A
SRVE0161I: IBM
WebSphere Application Server - Web
Container. Copyright IBM Corp.
1998-2001
[5/14/03 10:32:56:016 EDT] 67195e54 ServletEngine A
SRVE0162I: Servlet
Specification Level: 2.2
[5/14/03 10:32:56:016 EDT] 67195e54 ServletEngine A
SRVE0163I:
Supported JSP Specification Level: 1.1
```

```
[5/14/03 10:32:56:172 EDT] 67195e54 ServletEngine A
SRVE0167I: Session
Manager is Configured - Initializing...
[5/14/03 10:32:56:312 EDT] 67195e54 CacheManager  A
DYNA0011E: Servlet
cache file dynacache.xml not found; caching is
disabled
[5/14/03 10:32:56:391 EDT] 67195e54 ServletEngine A
SRVE0169I: Loading
Web Module: IBM Universal Test Client.
[5/14/03 10:32:56:906 EDT] 67195e54 WebGroup      I
SRVE0091I:
[Servlet LOG]: JSP 1.1 Processor: init
[5/14/03 10:32:56:938 EDT] 67195e54 WebGroup      I
SRVE0091I:
[Servlet LOG]: SimpleFileServlet: init
[5/14/03 10:32:57:297 EDT] 67195e54 ServletEngine A
SRVE0169I: Loading
Web Module: RPM Open Message Usage.
[5/14/03 10:32:57:703 EDT] 67195e54 WebGroup      I
SRVE0091I:
[Servlet LOG]: JSP 1.1 Processor: init
[5/14/03 10:32:57:703 EDT] 67195e54 WebGroup      I
SRVE0091I:
[Servlet LOG]: SimpleFileServlet: init
[5/14/03 10:32:57:734 EDT] 67195e54 WebGroup      I
SRVE0091I:
[Servlet LOG]: InvokerServlet: init
[5/14/03 10:32:57:844 EDT] 67195e54 HttpTransport A
SRVE0171I:
Transport http is listening on port 8,083.
[5/14/03 10:32:57:922 EDT] 67195e54 Server        A
WSVR0023I: Server
Default Server open for e-business
[5/14/03 10:33:34:438 EDT]  8275e5a WebGroup      I
SRVE0091I:
[Servlet LOG]: MsgSearch: init
java.lang.ArrayIndexOutOfBoundsException: 498
 at
org.apache.xml.dtm.ref.DTMManagerDefault.release(DTMM
anagerDefault.java(Compiled
Code))
 at
org.apache.xpath.XPathContext.release(XPathContext.ja
va:227)
 at
org.apache.xpath.objects.XRTreeFrag.destruct(XRTreeFr
ag.java:192)
 at
org.apache.xpath.objects.XRTreeFrag.finalize(XRTreeFr
ag.java:142)
```

```
   at
java.lang.ref.Finalizer.invokeFinalizeMethod(Native
Method)
   at
java.lang.ref.Finalizer.runFinalizer(Finalizer.java(C
ompiled
Code))
   at
java.lang.ref.Finalizer$FinalizerThread.run(Finalizer
.java(Compiled
Code))
   at
java.lang.ref.Finalizer$FinalizerThread.run(Finalizer
.java(Compiled
Code))
org.apache.xml.utils.WrappedRuntimeException:
d:\Program
Files\IBM\WebSphere Studio\RPMOpen_MsgUsage\Web
Content\temp\400\AbstractMessageData.xsd (Too many
open files)
   at
org.apache.xml.dtm.ref.DTMManagerDefault.getDTM(DTMMa
nagerDefault.java(Compiled
Code))
   at
org.apache.xpath.SourceTreeManager.parseToNode(Source
TreeManager.java(Compiled
Code))
   at
org.apache.xpath.SourceTreeManager.parseToNode(Source
TreeManager.java(Compiled
Code))
   at
org.apache.xpath.SourceTreeManager.getSourceTree(Sour
ceTreeManager.java(Compiled
Code))
   at
org.apache.xalan.templates.FuncDocument.getDoc(FuncDo
cument.java(Compiled
Code))
   at
org.apache.xalan.templates.FuncDocument.execute(FuncD
ocument.java(Compiled
Code))
   at
org.apache.xpath.XPath.execute(XPath.java(Compiled
Code))
   at
org.apache.xalan.templates.ElemWithParam.getValue(Ele
mWithParam.java(Compiled
Code))
```

```
 at
org.apache.xalan.templates.ElemCallTemplate.execute(E
lemCallTemplate.java(Compiled
Code))
 at
org.apache.xalan.transformer.TransformerImpl.executeC
hildTemplates(TransformerImpl.java(Compiled
Code))
 at
org.apache.xalan.templates.ElemIf.execute(ElemIf.java
(Compiled
Code))
 at
org.apache.xalan.transformer.TransformerImpl.executeC
hildTemplates(TransformerImpl.java(Compiled
Code))
 at
org.apache.xalan.templates.ElemTemplate.execute(ElemT
emplate.java(Compiled
Code))
 at
org.apache.xalan.templates.ElemCallTemplate.execute(E
lemCallTemplate.java(Compiled
Code))
 at
org.apache.xalan.transformer.TransformerImpl.executeC
hildTemplates(TransformerImpl.java(Compiled
Code))
 at
org.apache.xalan.templates.ElemIf.execute(ElemIf.java
(Compiled
Code))
 at
org.apache.xalan.transformer.TransformerImpl.executeC
hildTemplates(TransformerImpl.java(Compiled
Code))
 at
org.apache.xalan.templates.ElemTemplate.execute(ElemT
emplate.java(Compiled
Code))
 at
org.apache.xalan.templates.ElemCallTemplate.execute(E
lemCallTemplate.java(Compiled
Code))
 at
org.apache.xalan.transformer.TransformerImpl.executeC
hildTemplates(TransformerImpl.java(Compiled
Code))
 at
org.apache.xalan.transformer.TransformerImpl.transfor
mToRTF(TransformerImpl.java(Compiled
```

```
Code))
   at
org.apache.xalan.templates.ElemWithParam.getValue(Ele
mWithParam.java(Compiled
Code))
   at
org.apache.xalan.templates.ElemCallTemplate.execute(E
lemCallTemplate.java(Compiled
Code))
   at
org.apache.xalan.transformer.TransformerImpl.executeC
hildTemplates(TransformerImpl.java(Compiled
Code))
   at
org.apache.xalan.templates.ElemLiteralResult.execute(
ElemLiteralResult.java(Compiled
Code))
   at
org.apache.xalan.transformer.TransformerImpl.executeC
hildTemplates(TransformerImpl.java(Compiled
Code))
   at
org.apache.xalan.templates.ElemLiteralResult.execute(
ElemLiteralResult.java(Compiled
Code))
   at
org.apache.xalan.transformer.TransformerImpl.executeC
hildTemplates(TransformerImpl.java(Compiled
Code))
   at
org.apache.xalan.transformer.TransformerImpl.applyTem
plateToNode(TransformerImpl.java:2012)
   at
org.apache.xalan.transformer.TransformerImpl.transfor
mNode(TransformerImpl.java:1175)
   at
org.apache.xalan.transformer.TransformerImpl.transfor
m(TransformerImpl.java:642)
   at
org.apache.xalan.transformer.TransformerImpl.transfor
m(TransformerImpl.java:1092)
   at
org.apache.xalan.transformer.TransformerImpl.transfor
m(TransformerImpl.java:1070)
   at
com.rpm.ui.msgusage.core.Documentation.SaveDocs(Docum
entation.java:161)
   at
com.rpm.ui.msgusage.core.server.MsgSearch.doPost(MsgS
earch.java:340)
   at
```

```
javax.servlet.http.HttpServlet.service(HttpServlet.ja
va:760)
  at
javax.servlet.http.HttpServlet.service(HttpServlet.ja
va:853)
  at
com.ibm.servlet.engine.webapp.StrictServletInstance.d
oService(ServletManager.java:827)
  at
com.ibm.servlet.engine.webapp.StrictLifecycleServlet.
_service(StrictLifecycleServlet.java:167)
  at
com.ibm.servlet.engine.webapp.IdleServletState.servic
e(StrictLifecycleServlet.java:297)
  at
com.ibm.servlet.engine.webapp.StrictLifecycleServlet.
service(StrictLifecycleServlet.java:110)
  at
com.ibm.servlet.engine.webapp.ServletInstance.service
(ServletManager.java:472)
  at
com.ibm.servlet.engine.webapp.ValidServletReferenceSt
ate.dispatch(ServletManager.java:1012)
  at
com.ibm.servlet.engine.webapp.ServletInstanceReferenc
e.dispatch(ServletManager.java:913)
  at
com.ibm.servlet.engine.webapp.WebAppRequestDispatcher
.handleWebAppDispatch(WebAppRequestDispatcher.java:67
8)
  at
com.ibm.servlet.engine.webapp.WebAppRequestDispatcher
.dispatch(WebAppRequestDispatcher.java:331)
  at
com.ibm.servlet.engine.webapp.WebAppRequestDispatcher
.forward(WebAppRequestDispatcher.java:117)
  at
com.ibm.servlet.engine.srt.WebAppInvoker.doForward(We
bAppInvoker.java:134)
  at
com.ibm.servlet.engine.srt.WebAppInvoker.handleInvoca
tionHook(WebAppInvoker.java:239)
  at
com.ibm.servlet.engine.invocation.CachedInvocation.ha
ndleInvocation(CachedInvocation.java:67)
  at
com.ibm.servlet.engine.invocation.CacheableInvocation
Context.invoke(CacheableInvocationContext.java:106)
  at
com.ibm.servlet.engine.srp.ServletRequestProcessor.di
spatchByURI(ServletRequestProcessor.java:154)
```

```
at
com.ibm.servlet.engine.oselistener.OSEListenerDispatc
her.service(OSEListener.java:315)
at
com.ibm.servlet.engine.http11.HttpConnection.handleRe
quest(HttpConnection.java:60)
at
com.ibm.ws.http.HttpConnection.readAndHandleRequest(H
ttpConnection.java:323)
at
com.ibm.ws.http.HttpConnection.run(HttpConnection.jav
a:252)
at
com.ibm.ws.util.CachedThread.run(ThreadPool.java:137)
[5/14/03 10:34:55:547 EDT]   8275e5a SystemOut      U
java.lang.Exception: Save document error:
org.apache.xalan.res.XSLTErrorResources
java.lang.Exception: Save document error:
org.apache.xalan.res.XSLTErrorResources
at
com.rpm.ui.msgusage.core.Documentation.SaveDocs(Docum
entation.java:178)
at
com.rpm.ui.msgusage.core.server.MsgSearch.doPost(MsgS
earch.java:340)
at
javax.servlet.http.HttpServlet.service(HttpServlet.ja
va:760)
at
javax.servlet.http.HttpServlet.service(HttpServlet.ja
va:853)
at
com.ibm.servlet.engine.webapp.StrictServletInstance.d
oService(ServletManager.java:827)
at
com.ibm.servlet.engine.webapp.StrictLifecycleServlet.
_service(StrictLifecycleServlet.java:167)
at
com.ibm.servlet.engine.webapp.IdleServletState.servic
e(StrictLifecycleServlet.java:297)
at
com.ibm.servlet.engine.webapp.StrictLifecycleServlet.
service(StrictLifecycleServlet.java:110)
at
com.ibm.servlet.engine.webapp.ServletInstance.service
(ServletManager.java:472)
at
com.ibm.servlet.engine.webapp.ValidServletReferenceSt
ate.dispatch(ServletManager.java:1012)
at
com.ibm.servlet.engine.webapp.ServletInstanceReferenc
```

```
e.dispatch(ServletManager.java:913)
 at
com.ibm.servlet.engine.webapp.WebAppRequestDispatcher
.handleWebAppDispatch(WebAppRequestDispatcher.java:67
8)
 at
com.ibm.servlet.engine.webapp.WebAppRequestDispatcher
.dispatch(WebAppRequestDispatcher.java:331)
 at
com.ibm.servlet.engine.webapp.WebAppRequestDispatcher
.forward(WebAppRequestDispatcher.java:117)
 at
com.ibm.servlet.engine.srt.WebAppInvoker.doForward(We
bAppInvoker.java:134)
 at
com.ibm.servlet.engine.srt.WebAppInvoker.handleInvoca
tionHook(WebAppInvoker.java:239)
 at
com.ibm.servlet.engine.invocation.CachedInvocation.ha
ndleInvocation(CachedInvocation.java:67)
 at
com.ibm.servlet.engine.invocation.CacheableInvocation
Context.invoke(CacheableInvocationContext.java:106)
 at
com.ibm.servlet.engine.srp.ServletRequestProcessor.di
spatchByURI(ServletRequestProcessor.java:154)
 at
com.ibm.servlet.engine.oselistener.OSEListenerDispatc
her.service(OSEListener.java:315)
 at
com.ibm.servlet.engine.http11.HttpConnection.handleRe
quest(HttpConnection.java:60)
 at
com.ibm.ws.http.HttpConnection.readAndHandleRequest(H
ttpConnection.java:323)
 at
com.ibm.ws.http.HttpConnection.run(HttpConnection.jav
a:252)
 at
com.ibm.ws.util.CachedThread.run(ThreadPool.java:137)
```

A: What you need to do is to close all your streams in a final block, e.g.

code:
```
Source xslSource = new StreamSource(stylesheet);
TransformerFactory transFact =
TransformerFactory.newInstance();
Templates templates =
transFact.newTemplates(xslSource);
```

```java
for (int i=0; i<msgs.length; i++)
{
   File htmFile = new File(toPath, msgs + "_v" +
version + ".htm");
   File xsdFile = new File(msgPath, msgs + ".xsd");

   if (!htmFile.exists())
   {
       StreamSource sourceXSD = new
StreamSource(xsdFile);
       StreamResult resultHTM = new
StreamResult(htmFile);
       Transformer trans =
templates.newTransformer();
       trans.setParameter("docpath",
msgPath.getAbsolutePath() +
           System.getProperty("file.separator"));

       trans.transform(sourceXSD,
resultHTM);   <----------------FAILS

//**********Preferable close in a finally block
**********
       sourceXSD.close();
       resultHTM.close();
   }
}

File[] docs = toPath.listFiles();
//Also make sure you close any Streams you open in
your
//BatchDistributionUtil.zipFiles method

BatchDistributionUtil.zipFiles(docs, new File(toPath,
"documentation.zip"));
```

Question 60: WAS50 JMS IllegalStateException calling setMessageListener

In WAS 5.0, I'm using the embedded JMS Provider. I have a client application trying to talk to the bean. I can get the initial context, topic factory and topics, but I get the following error when the client tries to talk to the bean:

```
javax.jms.IllegalStateException: Method
setMessageListener not permitted
    at
com.ibm.ejs.jms.JMSCMUtils.methodNotPermittedExceptio
n(JMSCMUtils.java:200)
    at
com.ibm.ejs.jms.JMSMessageConsumerHandle.setMessageLi
stener(JMSMessageConsumerHandle.java:199)
    at
com.metamatrix.common.messaging.JMSMessageBus.addList
ener(JMSMessageBus.java:108)
    at
com.metamatrix.common.messaging.VMMessageBus.addListe
ner(VMMessageBus.java:79)
    at
com.metamatrix.platform.registry.MetaMatrixRegistryIm
pl.init(MetaMatrixRegistryImpl.java:100)
    at
com.metamatrix.platform.registry.MetaMatrixRegistryIm
pl.<init>(MetaMatrixRegistryImpl.java:76)
    at
com.metamatrix.platform.registry.MetaMatrixRegistryCo
ntrollerImpl.<init>(MetaMatrixRegistryControllerImpl.
java:39)
    at
com.metamatrix.platform.registry.MetaMatrixVMRegistry
.initialize(MetaMatrixVMRegistry.java:58)
    at
com.metamatrix.platform.registry.MetaMatrixVMRegistry
.getController(MetaMatrixVMRegistry.java:77)
    at
com.metamatrix.platform.registry.MetaMatrixVMRegistry
.registerVMController(MetaMatrixVMRegistry.java:251)
    at
com.metamatrix.platform.vm.controller.AppServerVMCont
roller.init(AppServerVMController.java:101)
    at
com.metamatrix.platform.security.api.beans.LogonAPIBe
an.ejbCreate(LogonAPIBean.java:67)
```

```
    at java.lang.reflect.Method.invoke(Native Method)
    at
com.ibm.ejs.container.StatelessBeanO.<init>(Stateless
BeanO.java:126)
    at
com.ibm.ejs.container.CMStatelessBeanO.<init>(CMState
lessBeanO.java:53)
    at
com.ibm.ejs.container.CMStatelessBeanOFactory.create(
CMStatelessBeanOFactory.java:40)
    at
com.ibm.ejs.container.EJSHome.createBeanO(EJSHome.jav
a:566)
    at
com.ibm.ejs.container.EJSHome.createBeanO(EJSHome.jav
a:653)
    at
com.ibm.ejs.container.activator.UncachedActivationStr
ategy.atActivate(UncachedActivationStrategy.java:78)
    at
com.ibm.ejs.container.activator.Activator.activateBea
n(Activator.java:518)
    at
com.ibm.ejs.container.EJSContainer.preInvoke_internal
(EJSContainer.java:2522)
    at
com.ibm.ejs.container.EJSContainer.preInvoke(EJSConta
iner.java:2259)
    at
com.ibm.ejs.container.EJSContainer.preInvoke(EJSConta
iner.java:2245)
    at
com.metamatrix.platform.security.api.EJSRemoteStatele
ssLogonAPIHome_4996d5f4.getEncryptor(Unknown Source)
    at
com.metamatrix.platform.security.api._LogonAPI_Stub.g
etEncryptor(_LogonAPI_Stub.java:658)
    at
com.metamatrix.platform.util.MetaMatrixController.che
ckAppServer(MetaMatrixController.java:176)
```

It appears that some type of permission must be set, but I've tried the topic factory J2C authentication, global security and tried adding permissions in the integral-jms-authorizations.xml file. But it seems I haven't hit the right combination.

Is there a solution for this?

A: You must use the MQ Series to solve your problem. In the J2EE, it says that:

Specification for an application server to allow
setMessageListener to be called from within the web container.
The reason WebSphere does not permit its use, despite the fact
that the WebSphere web container does allow threads to be spun
off, is because the asynchronous nature of this call interferes
with the management (sharing, pooling etc.) of the JMS
connection
by both the EJB and web containers.

Because of the wording of the specification, use of this method is
not portable and, indeed, the restriction has been tightened up in
the draft J2EE 1.4 specification:

"The following methods may only be used by application
components executing in the application client container:

```
- javax.jms.Session method setMessageListener
- javax.jms.Session method getMessageListener
- javax.jms.Session method run
- javax.jms.QueueConnection method
createConnectionConsumer
- javax.jms.TopicConnection method
createConnectionConsumer
- javax.jms.TopicConnection method
createDurableConnectionConsumer
- javax.jms.MessageConsumer method getMessageListener
- javax.jms.MessageConsumer method setMessageListener
- javax.jms.Connection method setExceptionListener
- javax.jms.Connection method stop
- javax.jms.Connection method setClientID
```

A J2EE container may throw a JMSException (if allowed by the
method) if the application component violates these
restrictions."

Question 61: Websphere Application Server Express V5 for iSeries

Has any had problems accessing the "Create New Express Server" option in the HTTP Admin section? I have been following the procedures in the WASE for iSeries Redbook and have been running with the initial setup with no problems.

When the Redbook gets to the section stating to access the iseries admin link (http://youriseries:2001), I can login with qsecofr here but when accessing the setup tab I do not get the option to "Create New Express Server".

I have applied the WS Group ptf and latest CUM, although not all the group ptfs could be applied due to pre-requisites. Perhaps this is where I am going wrong. Is there anyone who has successfully installed WS on an iSeries successfully whose WS Group PTFs were all installed?

A: To install the WAS Express on an iSeries with OS/400 V5R1M0, you need to install some PTFs before the installation of WebSphere. You need to do the following steps:

1. Be sure to have installed the following OS products:
   - 5722SS1 Option 18
   - 5722SS1 Option 34
   - 5722DG1 IBM HTTP Server
   - 5722JC1 Toolbox for Java
   - 5722JV1 Option *Base Developer Kit for Java
   - 5722JV1 Option 5 Java Developer Kit 1.3

2. You need to install the following groups of PTF:

   - SF99156 (HTTP, last level recommended. I had level 12)
   - SF99501 (DB. I had level 11)
   - SF99069 (Java, last level recommended. I had level 15)

3. Install WebSphere Application Server Express

4. Install PTF SF99270 (last level recommended);

5. You need to install additional PTF for WAS Express SI07518;

6. You need to install additional PTF for IBM Toolbox for Java, needed to WAS Express SI06156.

Question 62: Data source Problem WS 5

I installed WS Application server 5 and trying to run my application using jdbc data source. I created the data source as per the document but still am not able to run it successfully. It throws some exceptions -- error code : DSRA9002E .

What can I do to fix this?

A: It matters what type of data source you defined. If your EAR is J2EE 1.2-compliant, you need a "version 4" type data source. If your EAR is J2EE 1.3-compliant, you need the regular (Version 5) datasource. Also, make sure you are using a supported driver.

Question 63: Deploying JSP and Javabeans on WAS4.0

I am fairly new to WAS4.0 and am having difficulties in deploying my web application on WAS4.0. The application is running on Tomcat. It uses JSP, Java Beans only (no ejbs and servlets). Oracle8i is the back end.

What are the steps involved in deploying the application, configuring the web.xml file and also the URL to access my, say index.jsp file?

I am not using any deployment tools apart from AAT of WAS4.0. But I may use one if you recommend it and is available on site for download.

A: Check out your WSAD (WebSphere Studio Application Developer). This will actually allow you to debug on a test server running inside WSAD. After that, you can choose to bundle to and ear file. It will do most of the defining you need.

Question 64: Deploying application using scripting and specify classpath

I need to deploy my ear file in websphere 5.0 from the command line and I think I should use "$AdminApp install" for that. I would also like to specify additional classpath for the JVM settings and some custom properties and custom service. Could someone help me how can I do that?

A: Check out the following links for your problem:

Check out the IBM infocenter
http://publib7b.boulder.ibm.com/webapp/wasinfo1/in dex.jsp?deployment=ApplicationServer&lang=en

Quote:

Here is a quick way to deploy Web components, such as servlets and JSP files. This is not recommended as an official development method. It is provided so that you can sample the product functionality.

In summary, deploy Web components quickly by dropping the individual files into the directory structure of the default application installed by the product. This procedure relies on the Invoker servlet provided by the product. This servlet, enabled by default, lets you access deployed servlets by classname.

For recommended methods of developing and deploying Web application components, see Using Web applications.

Steps for this task:

1. If deploying a servlet, first compile your servlet.
2. Copy the servlet or JSP class file into the directory of the default application.
3. A servlet is placed in the directory:
install_root/installedApps/<cell_name>/DefaultApplication.ear /DefaultApplication.war/WEB-INF/classes.If your servlet has a package statement, then create a subdirectory in the above directory for each level in your package statement.

A JSP file is placed in the directory:

install_root/installedApps/<cell_name>/DefaultApplication.ear
/DefaultApplication.war
Open a browser window and request your servlet or JSP file.
The URL is:
http://your_host_name:9080/servlet/class_namewhere
class_name is the Java class implementing the servlet or JSP file.

End of quote.

Other links:

wsadmin
http://publib7b.boulder.ibm.com/wasinfo1/en/info/ae/ae/rxml_commandline.html

Shared Libraries using wsadmin
http://publib7b.boulder.ibm.com/wasinfo1/en/info/ae/ae/rxml_library.html

Question 65: Running Admin as non root (AIX) in WAS 5

I have to install WAS 5 (on AIX) and would like to know how to enable other users to run the Admin console and make sure they run under their own ID and not as root (as is the default). Also I am using WAS Deployment Manager but I do not know what changes I have to make there.

What can I do to fix this?

A: Try using a custom User Registry and establishing the admin credentials there. You might want to look at this for guidance. It may not cover 5 but it's worth a shot.

6.6.a.1: Running the product servers and consoles as non-root

in the InfoCenter
Found at:
http://mainframeforum.com/archive/1047/2002/1/749 17

Infocenter topic is:
http://www7b.software.ibm.com/wsdd/WASInfoCenter /infocenter/wasa_content/0606a01.html

Question 66: servlet 2.3 api in Websphere 4

Can I make use of the servlet filters in websphere 4? If so, how? I wanted to use the filters to compress my response data.

A: WAS 4 uses Servlet API 2.2. The WebSphere InfoCenter uses HTML 4.0, Cascading Style Sheets (CSS), JavaScript, and Java applets to provide advanced navigation features for a variety of computing platforms, such as Windows and UNIX.

Question 67: IBM HTTP Server ssl configuration problem

I am having trouble with the ssl configuration on the IHS 1.3.19.3, platform Solaris8. On one of our server, the ssl configuration works fine, i.e., I can access the server using https, if given in httpd.conf like this:

```
LoadModule ibm_ssl_module libexec/mod_ibm_ssl_128.so
Listen 443
SSLEnable
Keyfile /opt/ibm/gsk5/sslKeys/keys.kdb
```

Now if I try to give it this way

```
ServerName 1.2.3.4
SSLEnable
Port 443
SSLClientAuth none
SSLCipherSpec 39
SSLCipherSpec 3A
SSLCipherSpec 62
DocumentRoot /opt/IBMHTTPD/htdocs/en_US

Options +Includes
AllowOverride None
order allow,deny
allow from all

ErrorDocument 500 /redirect.html
ErrorLog /opt/IBMHTTPD/logs/error_log
TransferLog /opt/IBMHTTPD/logs/access_log
```

It gives error in apachecl configuration test command or if I try to start the IHS.

Syntax error on line 326 of /opt/IBMHTTPD/conf/httpd.conf:

Invalid command 'SSLEnable', perhaps mis-spelled or defined by a module not included in the server configuration. If I comment the line (as #SSLEnable), error remains the same, but with the next line of ssl config i.e. in my case 'SSLClientAuth none' and so on.

Is there a solution for this problem?

A: Something is wrong with your start and end tags. Start the admin server and edit it using the browser. In the /usr/HTTPServer/bin issue, the adminctl start then send a browser request to port 8008. You may need to set the user ID and password if you didn't use this before. Also, verify port 8008 in the admin.conf file.

Question 68: IBM HTTP server at windows 2000 startup

As I reboot the machine, the IBM HTTP server service cannot be started, no matter how I push it to open. It closes everytime and said that it is due to a windows internal error.

How do I fix this error?

A: You can get more information on what is going wrong by running apache.exe, which is in the server directory (C:\IBMHTTPServer) by default. When you run this file, you will get a command-line box which will give you a more useful description of what has gone wrong. It will close automatically after 30 seconds.

Question 69: websphere and the command line

Is there a way to list the application servers that websphere is managing from the command line?
Is there a way to get their status, i.e., if they are running from the command line? Is there a way to stop/start them from the command line? How do I fix this error?

A: You could use the TCL language to write scripts that would administrate the WebSphere Application Server. Invoke the WSCP mode of WebSphere and execute commands on the prompt, i.e.,

```
/WebSphere/AppServer/bin/wscp.sh
wscp> ApplicationServer list
```

The above command would list application servers available on your node. There are many more commands which could be executed from this mode. Create a file with a .tcl extension containing these commands and would help you execute a set of commands in one shot.

If you are in a UNIX environment, you could try this little script that basically just parses the ps command to find what WebSphere-related processes are running. Try it and see if you like it:

```
#!/usr/bin/ksh

echo "owner pid   ppid  process"
ps -ef | grep java | awk '
/com.ibm.ejs/ {
a=substr($0,index($0,"com.ibm.ejs.sm")+15)
if (index(a,"EJBServerProcess")>0) {
 b=substr(a,index(a,"EJBServerProcess")+17)
 c=substr(b,0,index(b,":")-1)
 a="server.ManagedServer " c
}
else {
 b=substr(a,0,index(a," ")-1)
 a=b
}
printf("%5s %d %d %s\n",$1,$2,$3,a );}'
```

Your mileage may vary, so see your dealer for details. You may need to adjust the values in the substring to return the correct process names.

Question 70: IBM WS Admin server doesn't start

I installed IBM WS Advanced Edition Version 4.x and DB2 7.2 as per instructions. I likewise updated to use Jdbc2.0. When I start WS Admin server , it does not start and giving the following error in the log.

How should I go about it?

```
[03.03.10 13:03:52:656 GMT+05:30] 149d5f19
DBMgr          F SMTL0026E: Failure to create a data
source: COM.ibm.db2.jdbc.DB2Exception: [IBM][CLI
Driver] SQL1013N  The database alias name or database
name "WAS40" could not be found.  SQLSTATE=42705

      at
COM.ibm.db2.jdbc.app.SQLExceptionGenerator.throw_SQLE
xception(SQLExceptionGenerator.java:174)
      at
COM.ibm.db2.jdbc.app.SQLExceptionGenerator.check_retu
rn_code(SQLExceptionGenerator.java:431)
      at
COM.ibm.db2.jdbc.app.DB2Connection.connect(DB2Connect
ion.java:445)
      at
COM.ibm.db2.jdbc.app.DB2Connection.<init>(DB2Connecti
on.java:354)
      at
COM.ibm.db2.jdbc.app.DB2ReusableConnection.<init>(DB2
ReusableConnection.java:66)
      at
COM.ibm.db2.jdbc.DB2PooledConnection.getConnection(DB
2PooledConnection.java:183)
      at
com.ibm.ejs.cm.pool.Connect0.<init>(Connect0.java:85)
      at
com.ibm.ejs.cm.pool.JDBC1xConnectionFactory.createCon
nection(JDBC1xConnectionFactory.java:42)
      at
com.ibm.ejs.cm.pool.ConnectionPool.createConnection(C
onnectionPool.java:914)
      at
com.ibm.ejs.cm.pool.ConnectionPool.createOrWaitForCon
nection(ConnectionPool.java:846)
      at
com.ibm.ejs.cm.pool.ConnectionPool.findFreeConnection
(ConnectionPool.java:764)
      at
```

```
com.ibm.ejs.cm.pool.ConnectionPool.findConnectionForT
x(ConnectionPool.java:676)
      at
com.ibm.ejs.cm.pool.ConnectionPool.allocateConnection
(ConnectionPool.java:610)
      at
com.ibm.ejs.cm.pool.ConnectionPool.getConnection(Conn
ectionPool.java:274)
      at
com.ibm.ejs.cm.pool.ConnectionPool.getConnection(Conn
ectionPool.java:269)
      at
com.ibm.ejs.cm.DataSourceImpl.getConnection(DataSourc
eImpl.java:99)
      at
com.ibm.ejs.sm.util.db.DBMgr.initialize(DBMgr.java:20
6)
      at
com.ibm.ejs.sm.server.AdminServer.initializeConnectio
nManager(AdminServer.java:1135)
      at
com.ibm.ws.runtime.Server.initializeRuntime0(Server.j
ava:943)
      at
com.ibm.ejs.sm.server.ManagedServer.initializeRuntime
0(ManagedServer.java:407)
      at
com.ibm.ejs.sm.server.AdminServer.initializeRuntime0(
AdminServer.java:1104)
      at
com.ibm.ws.runtime.Server.initializeRuntime(Server.ja
va:882)
      at
com.ibm.ejs.sm.server.AdminServer.main(AdminServer.ja
va:391)
      at java.lang.reflect.Method.invoke(Native Method)
      at
com.ibm.ws.bootstrap.WSLauncher.main(WSLauncher.java:
158)
```

A: This might happen because of security problems. Create a user called 'DB2Admin' and give it full administrative rights. When starting up the <u>websphere</u> admin program, websphere stores its own information into the db2 database. So you have to re-install websphere and at the point where it asks you for the location of db2, provide the username and password of the 'DB2ADMIN' username you created, and also the database name to where websphere must store its information. Websphere will then try to create this table, as specified in the installation. From

the trace above, it tries to connect to the database, but can't.
Also, maybe try to create the WAS40 table manually.
Try also the following: After installing WAS but before running
the Admin Server, execute /SQLLIB/java12/usejdbc2.bat

Another way is to acquire the enterprise version of DB2. It's
better to install DB2 first and then followed by the WebSphere
Application Server. But you have to uninstall first the existing
DB2 and WebSphere.

Question 71: Installation of WebSphere 5

I am trying to install websphere 5 on my gentoo 1.4rc1 box and I'm getting an error that stops the installation. I'm using the silent installation because I have no window manager. I edited the default optionfile to reflect my installation and then run:

```
./install -options ./options
```

where options is my optionfile. Then I get the following error message:

```
Setup.product.install,
com.ibm.ws.install.actins.LogMessageAction, msg1,
INST0051E: Unable to create user.
```

And then the install procedure quits.

I have tried a custom user and with root, but both fails. I'm running the installer as root.

How do I fix this?

A: First, you must create two users "mqm" and "mqbrkrs" and then create also two groups of the same name. Then add your root user to be a member of both the "mqm" and "mqbrkrs" groups.

In a full install with the MQ client, some get it running on Red Hat 8.0 only after creating the user "mqm" and these groups "mqm" and "mqbrkrs". Then place the root and and mqm into them.

Question 72: tag lib with websphere 3.5

I am a beginner and have a very basic question. Can I use Tag Libs with <u>WebSphere</u> version 3.5?

How do I fix this?

A: WAS 3.5 supports <u>JSP</u> 0.9 spec only. For taglib, you need to use JSP 1.0 or above. You can try installing some fix pack which would allow you to use taglib.

Question 73: Application Client machine setup and deployment

My company is considering the use of a standalone J2EE application client for a system within the company. We are trying to assess how difficult it is going to be to initially deploy the application client and to also deploy periodic updates to the application client. I have several questions and would appreciate anyone's assistance and wisdom:

1. What is required to be installed on a client to run an application client that is accessing EJBs on a Websphere 4.0 server? I am currently able to run my client by running the "launchClient.bat" file located in the \WEbsphere\AppServer\bin directory, but I can't seem to figure out how to launch the application client from an end-user machine that doesn't have the app server installed on it. Numerous searches on Google allude to the existence of a Websphere Appplication Client install CD, but I can't seem to locate any documentation of this on the IBM site.

2. Further, is it possible to create one JAR file that contains all the needed runtime and support software from #1 above as well as the application client (my code)? My motivation for this is that I want to use WebStart to deploy the application client and it appears that WebStart requires everything to be packaged into one JAR file. The end goal is for a new user to be able to use WebStart to click a link on a web browser and have everything needed to run the application client downloaded and installed.

A: Details about how to use the launchClient.bat for standalone J2EE application is contained in the info center for V4 at: http://www-3.ibm.com/software/webservers/appserv/infocenter.html.

Question 74: Oracle Data Source Driver

I am running Websphere Advance Single Server Edition
4.0. When I try to connect to my database using datasource, the
datasource returns a null value. I tried using classes12.zip in my
application /lib directory, but still I receive errors. I also put the
classes12.zip outside into the application server directory and it
is still incorrect. I have my data source point to both directories.

Do I need to install the Oracle 8i client to communicate with my
remote Oracle Database?

A: Yes, you need to install the Oracle 8i client to communicate
with your remote Oracle Database. You can refer to page 365 of
the WebSphere v4.0 Handbook regarding this.

The reason for the null pointer exception is that you might have
several jars that conflict with the class loaders and the
application server's classes.

The classes12.zip contains all the java classes that are needed to
communicate with the database even without the Oracle 8
client. You need the client only when you are running a thick or
oci drivers.

Question 75: Connection to AS400

I have a WebSphere Studio Advanced Edition 3.5 for Windows 2000 and I am trying to connect to an as400 using com.ibm.as400.access.AS400JDBCDriver. When I created the sql, I can see the data but when I run the servlet generated by the Database Wizard, I get the error: "java.lang.NullPointerException!!!..."

I have read that I have to change the servlet generated, which I did but it did not work.

Original Servlet:

```
<?xml version="1.0"?>
<!-- This file was generated by IBM WebSphere
Studio  using K:\Program
Files\WebSphere\Studio35\BIN\GenerationStyleSheets\V3
.5\JSP1.0\ServletModel\ServletConfig.xsl-->
<servlet>
  <markup-language>
    <ml-name>HTML</ml-name>
    <ml-mime>text/html</ml-mime>
    <page-list>
      <default-page>
        <uri>/Query1HTMLResults.jsp</uri>
      </default-page>

    </page-list>
  </markup-language>
  <code>Patty.Query1</code>
    <init-parameter
value="com.ibm.as400.access.AS400JDBCDriver"
name="driver"/>
    <init-parameter value="pwd" name="password"/>
    <init-parameter value="jdbc:as400://xxx"
name="URL"/>
    <init-parameter value="user" name="userID"/>
    <init-parameter value="jdbc/jdbcas400xxx"
name="dataSourceName"/>
</servlet>

Changed Servlet:
<?xml version="1.0"?>
<!-- This file was generated by IBM WebSphere
Studio  using K:\Program
Files\WebSphere\Studio35\BIN\GenerationStyleSheets\V3
.5\JSP1.0\ServletModel\ServletConfig.xsl-->
<servlet>
  <markup-language>
```

```
<ml-name>HTML</ml-name>
<ml-mime>text/html</ml-mime>
<page-list>
   <default-page>
      <uri>/Query1HTMLResults.jsp</uri>
   </default-page>

</page-list>
</markup-language>
<code>Patty.Query1</code>
   <init-parameter
value="com.ibm.db2.jdbc.app.DB2Driver"
name="driver"/>
   <init-parameter value="pwd" name="password"/>
   <init-parameter value="jdbc:db2:xxx" name="URL"/>
   <init-parameter value="user" name="userID"/>
   <init-parameter value="jdbc/jdbcdb2xxx"
name="dataSourceName"/>
</servlet>
```

Can anyone help me?

A: What you need to do is to download the JTOpen toolbox from
http://www-124.ibm.com/developerworks/opensource/jt400/ and then put it in the websphere\appserver\java (or jdk) folder. You will have to then add the path to the jt400.jar file in the command line for the jvm. This should be something like drive:\websphere\appserver\java\JTOpen\jt400.jar.

Question 76: WAS 4.0 and ConnPool

I am new to WAS and am playing around with it to compare using WAS to BEA and Oracle. I am having trouble trying to figure out how to setup a connection pool in WAS 4.0 (using it on Win 2K prof <u>server</u>).

I have setup a JDBC Driver Reference in the admin console but I can't find anything that has to do with a connection pool. The DB is MSSQL Server 2000. Do I have to write this myself?

A: If you are using a single server, select resources/the driver selection (i.e., Oracle <u>JDBC Driver</u>)/select data source. Under data source, select new/or modify. On the screen, you should then be able to review the connection pool's information.

Question 77: Silent install

Has anyone ever done a <u>WebSphere</u> v3.5 silent install on AIX? And if so, how could I change the install.script file and keep it from trying to execute a GUI display?

A: First, mount the cdrom (/cdrom) and on the CD, locate the file WebSphereInstallAIX.sh. Copy it to /tmp. Then create a response file in /tmp and call it WS_response.res (there is a sample of this on the CD like the one below:

```
IMAGE_DIR=/cdrom/usr/sys/inst.images
INSTALL_PLUGIN=X
INSTALL_IHS=X
INSTALL_APPLICATION=X
INSTALL_SAMPLES=X
INSTALL_ADMIN=X
INSTALL_INITIAL_CONFIG=X
USER_NAME=root
PASSWORD=<root password>
DB_TYPE    =DB2
DB_NAME    =<WebSphere Database Alias>
DB_USER    =<WebSphere Database UserName>
DB_PASSWORD=<WebSphere Database Password>
DB_HOME    =<DB2 database directory>
DB_URL=jdbc:db2:<WebSphere Database Name>
INSTALL_OLT=
```

Launch the install by:`cd /tmp`
`./WebSphereInstallAIX.sh WS_response.res`

Question 78: Keeping WAS 4.0 from serving up html pages

I have an odd situation where WAS 4.02 wants to serve up ALL files from the directory /site. However, this directory contains .html files as well as .jsp. Is there any way to have the .html files served up by the HTTP Server and not by WAS?

A: One way is to modify the security so that the .HTML files are available to the public. They would remain buried in the EAR file, but they would be displayed to the visitor even if they fail to login.

The following is an extract from the V4.0 Handbook:

"By default, WebSphere serves all the artifacts of an application, should they be static or dynamic. If your application uses a lot of static content, you may want to configure WebSphere so that the static content is served by the Web server instead. This comes at the expense of packaging the static contents of the application separately, and deploying them manually (there is no standard process to do this).

To do this, you must disable the File Serving Servlet. This can be done from the AAT, from the IBM Extensions tab of the Web Module Properties window, by un-checking the File serving enabled option.

You must then reinstall the application, and regenerate the plug-in configuration. To check that this has worked, you can look at the plugin-cfg.xml file, where you should see something similar to this, as opposed to a single rule that redirects all /webbank/* requests to WebSphere:

```
<UriGroup Name="webbankApplication/webbankWeb_URIs">
<Uri Name="/webbank/TransferServlet"/>
<Uri Name="/webbank/*.jsp"/>
<Uri Name="/webbank/*.jsv"/>
<Uri Name="/webbank/*.jsw"/>
<Uri Name="/webbank/j_security_check"/>
</UriGroup>
```

You should also configure the Web Server to recognize the /webbank URI. This can easily be done in Apache/IHS using an Alias directive... ."

Question 79: Installing websphere and displaying wrong code

I installed WebSphere 4.0 in the Japanese Win2k System and IBM DB2. Everything went okay including the DB2 and the http server. But when I started the administrator console, it displays the wrong character. The console is a java GUI, so I think there is something wrong in the JVM.
Maybe I should modify something in adminclien.bat file when I run the console.

How do I fix this?

A: In WebSphere 4.0.2, in the Japanese Environment, certain text strings on the AdminConsole GUI have not been translated correctly to the corresponding Japanese Values. So what you should do is to apply WebSphere efix PQ57024 to correct. Go and visit:

http://www-1.ibm.com/support/manager.wss?rs=0&rt=0&org=SW&doc=4001098

Question 80: Exception error

Does any body know the reason for the following error?

```
com.ibm.servlet.engine.srt.ClientClosedConnectionExce
ption
```

How could I catch it? Could somebody assist me on this?

A: The action "user closed/stoped/refreshed the webpage" results in a Broken Pipe Connection in WebServer because the user terminated the connection to the server before the entire response is sent. So, there is no active response object to write the response.

If you are using response.sendRedirect, you can catch this exception at the respond.sendRedirect method call.

Question 81: Creating Virtual Host in WebSphere Application Server

I am new to <u>WebSphere</u> AS. Could anyone tell me how to create a Virtual Host in WSAS? Also, XMLs could I edit to create a Virtual Host without using console? I want to write a Visual Basic code to create a Virtual Host in WebSphere Application Server.

A: This is what you should do:

1) Start WebSphere
2) Start the AdminConsole
3) Click on VirtualHost in the GUI
4) Add a default host of your choice.

To get the XML, there are a number of ways but the easiest is to get it from the Administration Console. Just click the Console menu and choose "Export to XML", etc.

Question 82: Setting KEEPGENERATED using Websphere console

How could I set KEEPGENERATED using Websphere console or any xml configuration file? I have added the following attributes statement in the ibm-web-ext.xmi:

```
"<jspAttributes name="keepgenerared" value =
"true"/>"
```

but it is not working. I am using websphere4.0.2.

How do I fix this?

A: It is not working because there is something wrong with your attributes. It should be

```
<jspAttributes xmi:id="JspAttribute_1"
name="keepgenerated" value="true"/>;
```

Question 83: GIOPVersionException

I have the following: Windows NT 4.0 Sp6a, Sql Server 7.0 / sp3, Websphere 4.0 Advanced Edition / fp3.

When I try to launch administration server, I get a specific error 10. Using adminserv.bat, I get a GIOPVersionException error. What does this error means?

This is what is displayed at the end of the log file:

End of extraction for F:/was40_aes_ptf_3/jdk_ptf_3.jar with no errors.

Basically this is what I did:

1) Installed jdk 1.1.3_4 but in a different logical drive because of space limitations on C:
2) Installed Webshere AE on the same logical drive with the system jdk. Then configured ws to use the native websphere jdk. Without rebooting, I performed the fixpack 3 upgrade specifying the path to the system path (same as JAVA_HOME environment variable). Then I rebooted.
3) Once I try to launch, I get the GIOPVersionException error.

Is there a step I am missing or performing wrong? Should I reboot after the initial websphere installation?

I also tried putting both the system jdk and WAS jdk in the JAVA_HOME within the environment variable but that did not work as well. Does it matter where you install the system jdk? I did not install it in the default directory due to space limitations.

A: GIOPVersionException normally means that the adminServer is running on a version of the JDK that is different to what is expected. If this happened after you installed PTF3, then it appears that the JDK upgrade failed. Check the jdk upgrade logs in c:\websphere\appserver\logs for more details.

A workaround is to install jdk 1.4 not 1.3 in the default JAVA_HOME directory.
1. Install j2ee sdk 1.4
2. Install Websphere AE. When prompted, use native IBM jdk.
3. Install fp3 and select use other JDK and then enter the path to the JAVA_HOME environment variable.

Question 84: Duplicate another server including WAS applications

I duplicated a new server from 'mksysb' tape including the WAS applications. I changed to a new server's IP address and host name. I also changed the HTTP Server's configuration to start HTTP server. But I could not start WebSphere Application Server even if I changed its configuration file admin.config. Later, I tried to recreate a new admin database and import original configuration. But I still couldn't start WAS server.
==================
Server Environment:
==================
OS: AIX 4.3.3 ML9
Java: 1.2.2
WebSphere Application Server: 3.5.0

How do I fix this?

A: The changed IP address and/or hostname of the machine should be updated in the following places:

DB2:

If the admin repository for WebSphere is also on the same machine, then you need to uncatalog the node and database and catalog them again with new IP address. This may need a machine restart. Connect to the admin repository database and then issue the following SQLs.

```
update ejsadmin.bindingbeantbl set name='newIP' where
name='oldIP'

update ejsadmin.bindingbeantbl set name='newHostname'
where name='oldHostname'

update ejsadmin.node_table set name='newHostname'
where name='oldHostname'
```

WebSphere configuration:
Edit sas.server.props file and replace all occurrences of the old hostname with the new hostname. Same changes must be made to sas.server.props.future, if it is not empty.

Restart Websphere.

Question 85: Scheduling a task in Websphere

I am interested in having a JSP page run during the first of every month. Is there anyway I can use Websphere to do this?

How do I fix this?

A: There are several ways to do this:

1. Use java.util.Timer and TimerTask (this API is available since JDK 1.3). Set one servlet as init-on-startup in your web.xml file, and then have this servlet run your Timer with the tasks you want. This timer can call anything, even your JSP.

2. Call URL from the UNIX script. Run this as a UNIX cron job. Similar can be done on Win 2K.

3. Use CustomService on WebSphere.

Question 86: The difference between direct jdbc connections and data sources

I would like to know the most important differences between direct jdbc connections and data sources from a transactional point of view.

How do I fix this?

A: The difference between direct jdbc connections and Data source is that Data sources are used to get a connection from the connection pool maintained by the Websphere Application Server where the creation of connection is not required. Take the connection from the pool, use it and close after completion. In direct jdbc connections, every time you create the connection, it hinders your application server performance.

Question 87: Role of Websphere

"Weblogic and <u>Websphere</u> - Both Weblogic and Websphere are designed to natively support the JSP and EJB architecture. They are both full-featured web servers that support a variety of server side architectures, including CGI-BIN and Java based solutions."

I got this explanation from internet. I'm a little bit confused here. Does Websphere include webserver also? I know some people are using Websphere as well as HTTP <u>Server</u>. I really appreciate if anybody explains the role of Websphere in web based applications.

How do I fix this?

A: WebSphere does include a webserver (at 9080 port by default), but to harness the production capabilities of the webserver, you are not supposed to use the built-in webserver of websphere. WAS does support many webserver like apache, IIS, and iplanet. You can install any of these and plug-in WAS with the <u>web server</u>.

Question 88: Convert to a WAR file

I have installed both WAS 3.5 Standard edition and Advanced edition. While reading the handbook, I've found out that both of them lack one task, that is, to convert a War file in the Console→ Tasks.

Why is this so?

A: IBM WebSphere Application Server Version 3.5 Fix Pack 2 (also known as Version 3.5.2) introduces support for WAR files. However, Fix Pack 2 has been designed to maintain compatibility with existing applications. As such, WAR files are only used as a deployment vehicle in Version 3.5.2. After a WAR file is installed into the server runtime, the WAR file itself is no longer used.

Question 89: Setting up a cluster

I am new to WebSphere and am having a problem trying to set
up something similar to a WebLogic cluster. I tried to set up a
server group but cannot get round-robin nor fail-over to
work. In WebLogic, I can be connected to one of the cluster
servers and if I shut the server I am on, I can be redirected to a
working server and session info would persist. In WebSphere, I
am unable to do this.

Is there something similar in WebSphere?

A: First thing you should do is to finalize your Application
Server build through the following steps:

1) Right click on it and create Model.
2) Set "Make xxxx a Clone" and "Recursively all instances". Also
name your Model. This is will now create a Clone and also
convert your existing Application Server to a clone of that Model.
To create another Clone, right click on the model. Click Create→
Clone and select Node.
You now have two Clones. Right click the Model and select Start
and this will start the two Clones together.

All WLM enabled Clients will now get an array of proxy stubs
which will have details pertaining to each of the Clones. The wlm
policy of Round-Robin etc. is set through the Advanced Tab of
the Model and Failover is automatic.

For more information on this see Chapter 17 of the 3.5 Handbook
available from www.redbooks.ibm.com

Question 90: Websphere 4.0 installation and install shield error

I am trying to install websphere app server 4.0 on win2k but I keep on seeing the message below, after staying at 99% of the install process.

WebSphere Application Server 4.0: _INS5576._MP - Application Error : The instruction at "0x01ee45b2" referenced memory at "0x0000000c". The memory could not be "read".
Click on OK to terminate the program.

How do I fix this?

A: This error can occur during the launching of the installation shield. The error may be displayed after the Installation Shield appears in the bottom right corner of the screen and has reached 99%.

Performing the following steps will correct this problem.

STEP 1. Check Auto insert Notification, Reserved Drive Letters assignment and DMA settings of the DVD-ROM drive.

1. Click Start select Settings and Control Panel
2. Double click on the System icon
3. Select the Device Manager tab
4. Click the + (plus sign) next to CD-ROM to expand the branch
5. Click on the DVD drive listed in this branch
6. Click the Properties button
7. Select the Settings tab
8. Set reserved drive letters - both boxes should read the same - as the current drive letter assignment
9. Remove the tick from the Auto Insert Notification box
10. If there is a tick in DMA (Direct Memory Access) - remove it, if there is not place a tick there
11. Click OK
12. Close all open windows
13. Restart Windows

STEP 2. Set optimize access pattern setting of the DVD-ROM drive.

1. Click on Start select Settings and Control Panel
2. Double click on the System icon
3. Click the Performance tab
4. Click the File System button
5. Click the CD-ROM tab
6. Open the Optimize access pattern for drop down menu and select "No Read Ahead"
7. Press the Apply button
8. Close all open windows
9. Restart Windows

STEP 3. Clear the contents of the c:\WebSphere\AppServer directory to eliminate any file conflicts.

1. Open the Recycle Bin and from its File Menu select Empty Recycle Bin, confirm deletion by clicking Yes
2. Double click on My Computer icon to open it
3. Double click on C:\
4. Double click on the Windows folder
5. Double click on the Temp folder
6. Open the Edit Menu and select the Select All option
7. Open the File Menu and select the Delete option
8. Click Yes to any on-screen messages to confirm deletion
9. Return to the desktop

STEP 4. Disable all Anti-Virus software.

1. End all background programs, except for Explorer and Systray, individually from within the Close Program window by Pressing Ctrl ; Alt ; Del in this order, holding down all keys simultaneously, then releasing all keys after pressing Del.
2. Once in the Close Program window click on the name of the program so that it is highlighted and click the End Task button. (If, in response another window displays stating that the program is busy or waiting for input, click the End Task in that window as well)
3. Repeat the 2 steps above for all programs until only Explorer and Systray (Systray may not be running on your system) remain, click Cancel to finish.

STEP 5. Re-install WebSphere.

Question 91: Using a CMP MS Access database on Win2000 & WAS 4.0

I'm a relative beginner with WAS 4.0. I have installed the trial software on Win2000 and it all seems to be OK. I'm trying to work out how to configure a server to access a Jet/MS Access database. I'm using Access as a trial db for the moment. The help/documentation indicates that I should setup a "datasource" on a server configuration. Is this correct? If so, the documents concentrate on DB2 datasources. How would I set up a datasource to Access using the jdbc/odbc bridge?

A: Connection pooling is only available for Relational Databases that support JDBC. Therefore, the only Microsoft Database Supported under WebSphere is "Microsoft SQL Enterprise Edition (2000 & v7).

However, you can connect to ODBC Relational Databases using ODBC database using the Sun JDBC-to-ODBC bridge driver included in the Java Development Kit (JDK) or another vendor's ODBC driver.

The URL attribute specifies the location of the database. The driver attribute specifies the name of the driver to be used to establish the database connection.

If the database is an ODBC database, you can use an ODBC driver or the Sun JDBC-to-ODBC bridge included with the JDK. If you want to use an ODBC driver, refer to the driver documentation for instructions on specifying the database location (the url attribute) and the driver name.

In the case of the bridge, the URL syntax is jdbc:odbc:database. An example is:

url="jdbc:odbc:autos"
driver="sun.jdbc.odbc.JdbcOdbcDriver"

To enable the Application Server to access the ODBC database, use the ODBC Data Source Administrator to add the ODBC data source to the System DSN configuration. To access the ODBC Administrator, click the ODBC icon on the Windows NT Control Panel.

Also, just because a database has a JDBC Driver does not mean that it is supported as a CMP Datasource. Most Application Servers do a lot of optimizations for CMP and these will differ between RDMBS products. You will be pretty much guaranteed the top 3 (Oracle, SQL Server, and DB2) but I would highly doubt that Access is supported as a CMP source.

Question 92: Websphere and XML message

Can WebSphere MQ send an XML message?

A: WebSphere MQ doesn't concern itself with what is being sent in a given message, so the message data could be XML or any other format. However, the WebSphere MQ Integrator and WBI Event/Message Broker products have a built-in parser for processing XML messages.

Question 93: WebSphere MQ and server connection

Does the WebSphere MQ client need to be installed on the server in order for clients to connect to the server?

A: The WebSphere MQ client software does not need to be installed on the server in order for a client to connect to the queue manager. However, if you need to use a client locally on the queue manager machine, it must be installed.

Question 94: Return code 2033 on a Solaris server

I have an application that sends PCF commands to inquire channel status. This works fine on a Windows 2000 server, but on a Solaris server, I always get return code 2033 (MQRC_NO_MSG_AVAILABLE). What could be wrong?

A: The problem is very likely that the command server is not active on your Solaris server. On Windows, the command server is generally configured to start during queue manager startup. With the UNIX platforms, you must manually start the command server for each queue manager.

The syntax is strmqcsv qmgrname.

Question 95: Finding the directory entry for a created queue manager

I created a queue manager on MQSeries for AIX and I cannot find the directory entry for it. What is the directory and object naming convention for MQSeries for AIX?

A: The queue manager name can be up to 48 characters, but this does not automatically guarantee that this will be a valid or unique AIX directory name; therefore a directory name will be generated by AIX in a name transformation process. When a new name is generated, there is no simple relationship between the real and transformed names.

Certain rules are followed by MQ Series for naming the directory to come up with a valid name, such as:

1. Transform individual characters:
   a. . becomes !
   b. / becomes &

2. If the name is still not valid:
   a. Truncate it to eight characters
   b. Append a three character numeric suffix

This directory resides under /var/mqm/qmgrs.

Question 96: Error message "MSGS0200E: the broker DataFlowEngine return code was: 1"

I am running WebSphere Application Server 5.0.2 on Win2000 platform, but cannot get the embedded Broker to start, and the SystemOut.log file shows the error message "MSGS0200E: The Broker DataFlowEngine return code was: 1". What could be causing this error?

How do I fix this?

A: This failure could be caused by the fact that the WBI Event Broker or the WebSphere MQ Integrator product is installed on the same machine, but it is at the incompatible code level with the code level of WebSphere's embedded publish/subscribe (WEMPS) Broker. Check the Java Library Path shown in the SystemOut.log file to see if it includes the WMQI bin library ahead of the WEMPS\bin library. If this is the case, modify your PATH to remove the WMQI bin library and then start your WAS server.

Question 97: Asynchronous message listener and asynchronous queue receiver

I am trying to implement an asynchronous message listener in my Web component under WebSphere Application Server 5.0. I am not using message-driven bean. Instead, my listener class implements JMS MessageListener interface and the onMessage method. This message listener is then registered with my asynchronous queue receiver (consumer) by using the setMessageListener() method. I am unable to make my Web component run. At run time my application receives a javax.jms.IllegalStateException: Method setMessageListener not permitted.

What am I doing wrong? How do I fix this?

A: You seem to be running into the WebSphere Application Server 5.0 restriction resulting from WebSphere's strict implementation of J2EE 1.3 and EJB 2.0 specifications. Your only option is to use the Message Driven Bean or invoke your message listener in the Client container.

The J2EE 1.3 Specification document in the section "J2EE.6.7 Java Message Service (JMS) 1.0 Requirements" states as follows:

"Note that the JMS API creates threads to deliver messages to message listeners. The use of this message listener facility may be limited by the restrictions on the use of threads in various containers. In EJB containers, for instance, it is typically not possible to create threads. The following methods must not be used by application components executing in containers that prevent them from creating threads:

- javax.jms.Session method setMessageListener
- javax.jms.Session method getMessageListener
- javax.jms.Session method run
- javax.jms.QueueConnection method createConnectionConsumer
- javax.jms.TopicConnection method createConnectionConsumer
- javax.jms.TopicConnection method createDurableConnectionConsumer

- javax.jms.MessageConsumer method getMessageListener
- javax.jms.MessageConsumer method setMessageListener"

The above limitations are enforced in WAS 5.0 by throwing a javax.jms.IllegalStateException whenever any of the listed methods is called from the EJB or Web containers. Consequently, WAS 5.0 InfoCenter contains this explicit warning":

"Note: A MessageListener can only be used in the client container. (The J2EE specification forbids the use of the JMS MessageListener mechanism for the asynchronous receipt of messages in the EJB and Web containers.)"

See the following link for more details: WAS Version 5 InfoCenter: Designing an enterprise application to use JMS.

Question 98: AMQ6119 an internal MQSeries error

I am getting the message "AMQ6119 an internal MQSeries error has occurred - too many open files from shmat."

What might cause this problem?

How do I fix this?

A: If this is accompanied by an FDC file with Probe ID XY333013, this can be caused by not having enough file descriptors defined. Increase the number of file descriptors in /etc/system. Set

rlim_fd_max=4096
rlim_rd_cur=1024

If you still experience this problem, increase the soft limit, rlim_rd_cur to 2048.

Question 99: Error AMQ7077 – not authorized to run the command

I am having a problem with starting MQSeries 5.3 at bootup on Solaris. I have installed MQSeries and configured the groups so that root is part of the mqm group. I have created a startup script that runs at bootup to start MQ, i.e., strmqm, and I am getting an error AMQ7077 - not authorized to run the command. If I run the script manually after logging in as root, it works fine. I have confirmed that at bootup, the user being used is root.

How do I correct the problem?

A: The problem described is affecting Solaris and some Linux platforms. It can be circumvented by doing 'su' command to 'mqm' user before issuing 'strmqm' in the bootup script. So, the recommended way of starting queue manager from the bootup script would be via the following command:

```
su - mqm -c "/opt/mqm/bin/strmqm ${QMGRNAME}"
```

That way the 'root' user doesn't even have to be in the 'mqm' group.

Question 100: Error 2035 when using COD report

Why do I receive error 2035 when using COD report but not when using the COA report?

A: Confirmation on Arrival (COA) reports generated by the queue manager are put with the authority that was used when the message causing the report was put on the queue manager generating the report. It could be using the MCA authority which would make it successful.
Your Confirmation on Delivery (COD) report messages are put using the authority of the User Identifier in the MQMD of the message causing the report. You are getting the 2035 error because the UserIdentifier does not have authority to open and put to the ReplyToQueue.

Question 101: Two queue manager names on the same network

Can two queue manager names on the same network be identical?

A: While it is possible to have the two queue managers with identical names on the same network, it is not recommended. Failure to have unique queue manager names can result in duplicate message ID's. Also, if the names are not unique in a network of interconnected queue managers, queue managers won't be able to unambiguously identify the target queue manager for any given message which is sent.

References

http://en.wikipedia.org/wiki/IBM_WebSphere
http://www-306.ibm.com/software/integration/wbiserver/faq-43.html
http://www-306.ibm.com/software/integration/wbimodeler/faq/faq_51.html
http://www.tek-tips.com/threadminder.cfm?pid=831
http://www-304.ibm.com/jct09002c/isv/tech/faq/category.jsp?catId=401

Index

www.ingramcontent.com/pod-product-compliance
Lightning Source LLC
Chambersburg PA
CBHW071134050326
40690CB00008B/1463